getting into

Psychology
Courses

trotman

getting into

Psychology Courses

Maya Waterstone

Getting into Psychology Courses
Seventh edition

First published in 1994; second edition 1996; third edition 1999; fourth edition 2002; fifth edition 2004; sixth edition 2006; this seventh edition published in 2008 by Trotman Publishing a division of Crimson Publishing Ltd., Westminister House, Kew Road, Richmond, Surrey TW9 2ND

© Trotman Publishing 2008

Editorial and Publishing Team
Author Maya Waterstone
Advertising Sarah Talbot, Advertising Sales Director

British Library Cataloguing in Publication Data
A catalogue record for this book is available from the British Library

ISBN 978 1 84455 151 4

Typeset by NewGen Imaging

Printed and bound by The Cromwell Press, Trowbridge, Wiltshire

Contents

For up-to-date information on psychology courses go to
www.mpw.co.uk/getintopsych

About the author

Maya Waterstone is a Director of Studies and careers advisor at MPW London. She is a qualified Child and Adolescent counsellor. She has also written articles for a Religious Studies magazine and is a teacher of Religious Studies at both GCSE and A Level.

Acknowledgements

I am grateful for the help provided by Trotman Publishing who allowed us to bring the information that we had prepared over a number of years for MPW students to a wider readership, and to those who worked on the earlier ediotions, Thank your also to the British Psychology Society whose excellent website and range of publications made the job of writing this guide much easier, and to UCAS. I would also like to thank the admissions staff at the universities who provided the information on courses in Chapter 5, and James Burnett for his contribution to this book.

Maya Waterstone
January 2008

Introduction

For 2006 entry, 15,000 applicants applied for just over 13,000 places on psychology courses at UK universities. Of the 15,000 applicants, 12,000 were women and 3,000 were men. Psychology continues to be a very popular degree course option because it offers a number of well-defined career paths as well as being perceived by employers in general as being a valuable qualification, as it combines scientific analysis, mathematical skills and the requirement to be able to write coherent and structured essays.

Although there is not quite the pressure on psychology degree course places as there is for potential medics or vets, the application statistics show that applicants are certainly not guaranteed a place. Furthermore, many applicants have very clear ideas about which universities they wish to target (some of the most popular universities have up to 20 applications for every place) and so applicants need to think carefully about the strategies they are going to adopt in order to maximise their chances. This is why we have written this book: to give prospective psychology students advice about making a successful and convincing application.

About this book

Deciding what to study after A levels is a daunting task. There are already numerous books, guides and leaflets available to help you make your choice. So, why bother to write yet another? *Getting into Psychology Courses* is, as the title suggests, specifically for people wanting to do psychology at degree level. We hope it provides a clear and concise introduction to a subject which relatively few students do at school. It contains information on entry requirements, the length and content of the various courses on offer, and a little about the actual university psychology departments. It also provides some guidelines on making your UCAS application, writing your personal statement and preparing for an interview. If, after reading the following chapters, your decisions have been eased in any way, we will have achieved our goal.

This book is intended to complement, not replace, existing publications, many of which are included in the reading list at the end of the guide.

Details of entry requirements, courses, campus facilities, etc are constantly changing and, although the details in this guide are correct at the time of going to press, it is essential to check with UCAS and/or particular universities if you have any queries.

For up-to-date information on psychology courses go to
www.mpw.co.uk/getintopsych

01 Psychology and related careers

It is important to distinguish between the role of the psychologist and other professionals carrying out related work.

- **Psychiatrist**
  A medically trained doctor who chooses to specialise in mental health by taking the membership examinations of the Royal College of Psychiatry. As a consequence of their medical training, psychiatrists can prescribe drug treatments. They will often work as part of a team with clinical psychologists.
- **Psychotherapist**
  Works with both individuals and groups to provide long-term therapy. They will often encourage clients to reflect on their past experience and early development. In theory, graduates of any subject can become a psychotherapist by taking a lengthy training programme of supervised clinical practice and seminars and, in addition, undergoing personal therapy themselves.
- **Psychoanalyst**
  Bases his or her work on Freudian theory and tries to unearth the influence of the unconscious on clients' behaviour. Psychoanalysts work with individual clients in private practice rather than in paid employment. As with psychotherapy, the training period of at least four years includes the process of personal analysis.

Psychology, the study of people and how they act and think, is an increasingly popular subject of study with over 100 higher education institutions offering degree-level courses in the subject either as free-standing degree programmes in their own right or as modules in other combined programmes. Despite this growth in student places, there are still, however, some popular misconceptions about the content of degree programmes. They do not offer students the chance to spend three years studying the works of Freud. Nor do they enable you to see into other people's innermost thoughts.

On the contrary, psychology is taught as a scientific subject and students spend most of their time studying the results of research into human behaviour and the theories which are based on experimental findings. The aim of this introductory chapter is to give you an insight into some of the typical psychological research findings you are likely to study in the course of a degree programme. For more information about

1

psychology as a career, you should look at the British Psychological Society's (BPS) website: www.bps.org.uk.

Careers

According to Prospects, the UK's official graduate careers website, approximately 61% of psychology students who graduated from university in 2005 had found employment within six months of graduating. About 24% of 2005's graduates were undertaking further study (or combining study with work). The relatively high figure of psychology graduates continuing with their studies is an indication of the need to gain further qualifications (see page X) in order to practise as a psychologist. For the students going directly into employment, there was a wide range of destinations, finance, clerical and office work, managerial positions and teaching.

How long is a piece of string?

In 1955, the psychologist Solomon Asch set up an experiment in which he sat a group of people around a table and asked them, in turn, to state which of three lines (drawn on one card) was the same length as the single line shown on another card. So, A, B or C?

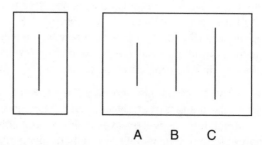

A   B   C

The answer is not as easy as it seems. In fact, the experiment was arranged so that all but one of the group were told beforehand to give the same, but incorrect, answer (ie A). The other person, the 'naive subject' who was not in on the act, was placed to answer last. Surprisingly, despite the simplicity of the task, the naive subject often gave the same wrong answer as his or her companions, preferring to conform than to stand out. It's amazing what peer pressure can do! 'So what?' I hear you cry, 'No one goes round asking complete strangers to judge the lengths of lines.'

In subsequent experiments, Asch found that the naive subject's response often varied with the composition of the group. If one other person deviated from the general consensus (even if he or she gave the other wrong answer), then the subject usually gave the correct response. If the subject was allowed to write his or her judgement on paper, the answer was always right and, if someone left the room before responding, the subject felt able to give the right answer (assuming, no doubt, that the absent person would have given the correct reply).

It seems, therefore, that a person's expressed thoughts and opinions are not necessarily what he or she secretly believes. The study was deliberately designed to be simple and unlike anything the naive subjects had previously experienced so that they could not refer to past events to guide their behaviour. In addition, there was no risk of some members being thought of as more 'expert' than others in the field of judging line length!

Therefore, if peer pressure could have such a profound effect in this simple task, imagine the implications for real-life situations. Many other researchers did similar studies, finding that the results varied according to factors such as how the subject rated his or her companions, whether the subject wanted to be accepted by them and wished to conform, or whether the subject felt superior to them and didn't care that they might be ridiculed for deviating from the general judgement, and so on.

■ Now you see it...

A good deal of experimental research in psychology has centred on the theme of perception in order to explain how we see and hear. One particular challenge facing psychologists was to account for the way visual illusions, such as the Muller-Lyer illusion below, achieve their effect. Why, for example, does the vertical line in A look longer than that in B?

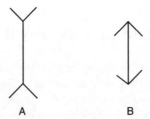

A   B

How can the brain interpret one set of signals in two different ways? One explanation, offered by a researcher called RL Gregory, suggests that the context in which a signal is seen, as well as one's expectations, are both highly influential in the interpretation of sensory signals (visual, audio and tactile). So, if a signal is incomplete, the gaps are filled by what you expect to see, hear or touch, rather than with what is really there. Research into this can provide valuable information on how perception normally happens and allows exploration of what can go wrong.

Again, there are far-reaching applications of the findings of such work. For example, if perception is influenced by suggestion and expectation, the gaps filled by the probable rather than the definite, surely the same is true of memory, raising the question: 'How reliable is eye-witness evidence?' Then there is the issue of artificial perception and intelligence – can a computer think or is it only as clever as the person who programs it?

Coming back to the lines, the way they appear is all to do with perspective. We are fooled into thinking that the 2D image on paper is a 3D phenomenon. Think of it in terms of a room. The vertical line in A is the far corner of a room and the diagonal lines represent the ceiling coming towards us. The diagram in B also shows the corner of a room, but this time it's the corner closest to us and the diagonal lines are the ceiling receding into the distance. Now, because the line in A represents a corner further away from us than the line in B, our brain amplifies the image falling on the retina of the eye to compensate for the extra distance, making it look longer than the line in B, which is not amplified. It's a bit like when you see a car on the horizon: you know that it looks tiny because it is a long way away and your brain makes the necessary adjustment to make it look 'car-sized'.

Therefore, perspective is normally useful to us, but the illusion arises if we use it when it is not needed (line A is NOT further away than line B). It's complicated but it is a handy tool to have; artists, architects and designers all make use of it when depicting 3D things on a flat piece of paper. Perspective is, however, a learned process. People who are deprived of seeing things in the distance – like some forest-dwelling tribes and those held in captivity for long periods – do not see things in perspective and, to them, both lines would look the same length.

■ It's not what you say, it's the way that you say it

Verbal communication is interesting for two reasons. Firstly, in association with the theories of speech: how do we learn? Do we plan exactly what to say before we say it or do we put the finishing touches to grammar and word order as we go along? (Think about the errors of speech, how we stumble over words, say them in the wrong order and then go back to make corrections, how we use plural verbs with a singular subject, and so on.) Those 'ums' and 'ahhhs' so common in everyday speech are pauses that allow planning time for the next segment of the sentence.

Secondly, in the way a message is given. How, and by whom, it is delivered can be as influential as its content. For example, is it more effective to speak first or second in a debate? Will the voters remember more of what they heard first or of what they heard most recently?

Indeed, do political campaigns really make a difference to voting behaviour? Is an attractive person more likely to be believed than a less attractive one? If not, perhaps spending so much money on media image is a waste of time. Maybe a voter will assure each party that it can rely upon his or her support, reserving his or her choice for the privacy of the polling booth (remember Asch and his lines)? The list is endless!

■ How do children think?

Swiss psychologist Jean Piaget earned international renown for his studies of children's intellectual development. As a result of his observations of their behaviour, he suggested that each child goes through a sequence of developmental stages up to the age of 12. One particular experiment characterised the child's thought processes at an early stage of their development and illustrates the process Piaget referred to as 'conservation'.

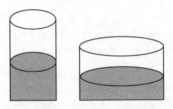

During the experiment he showed a child two identical glasses with equal amounts of liquid and asked the child to agree that they were the same in volume. Piaget then poured the liquid into glasses of different sizes, one tall and thin and the other shorter and wider than the other. Typically the pre-school child no longer agreed that the two glasses contained equal amounts of liquid, arguing that the taller glass had more liquid. At this stage in its cognitive development, the child centres on the appearance of the objects rather than accepting that the volume of the liquid is conserved.

This is simply one example of a lifetime of research into child development undertaken by Piaget. Some of his findings have been challenged by later researchers who have shown that infants in particular are more skilled, cognitively, than Piaget suggested. His ideas, however, have proved highly influential in showing the way that children's thought processes develop over time and have been widely incorporated into the training of teachers and educational psychologists.

If you are keen to find out more, there is a huge array of excellent introductory books on psychology, which will provide an overview of the subject as a whole.

■ Why is psychology so popular?

Overall, then, why is psychology such a popular subject for a first degree? There are several reasons.

- Potential students are attracted to a subject that gives them insights into human behaviour and most students of psychology have a basic interest in people.
- It is a particularly attractive subject for mature students who may already have touched on the subject during previous training. Business managers, nurses and social services staff may well have been introduced to some of the basic concepts in psychology and want to learn more.
- Psychology is a subject that can be seen to span both arts and science subjects. It attracts students who have broadly based interests and abilities, who do not want to be seen as either an 'arts' or a 'science' person.
- Finally, although the subject of psychology has been studied at university level for a century – the first professor of psychology was appointed in 1919 – it is still seen as a comparatively 'new' subject and because of the volume of research carried out around the world, students will be studying a subject in which the boundaries of knowledge are constantly changing.

What is more, as a result of the diverse applications of psychology in, for example, healthcare, sports psychology and organisational development, many new and exciting work opportunities are being created.

02 Degree programmes in psychology

When choosing a degree course in psychology there are several points to bear in mind. Firstly, degree programmes will vary in their emphasis. Some will offer a general but comprehensive grounding in the subject. Others will tend to specialise in one branch of psychology. Secondly, admission to courses is usually open to students irrespective of the AS or A level subjects or other qualifications they have studied.

However, some courses which lead to a Bachelor of Science (BSc) degree in psychology may favour students with science subjects, because of the scientific or experimental nature of the degree course and the ancillary or minor subjects you may be expected to take.

Degree programmes leading to a Bachelor of Arts (BA) degree may look favourably at applicants with arts A level subjects. The distinction between the two is an important one, because the titles of the awards may not only reflect differences in main course content but also in the choice of subsidiary courses you can take. Those studying for science-based courses may have option choices in neuroscience or physiology whereas those on arts-based programmes may have options in social or developmental psychology.

■ General or specialised?

Not all first degree programmes in psychology have the same aims. Some are intended to be general in nature, giving a broad and comprehensive overview of all aspects of psychology. Others, by contrast, will attempt to give a special emphasis to one aspect of the subject. You will soon see from the course listings which follow whether a course has a general or specific emphasis. Examples of specialised courses include Applied Psychology, Experimental Psychology, Occupational Psychology and Social Psychology. There can be some benefits in completing this kind of degree, particularly if you already know that this aspect of psychology interests you. On graduation, it may also enable you to gain advanced recognition by the relevant professional group or division of the British Psychological Society.

■ Single subject, joint or modular?

Most university departments of psychology will offer a **single Honours** degree in the subject, which means that your principal subject is psychology but that you may have to study other minor subjects in addition, which carry less weight in terms of marks and assessment.

In addition, there are numerous examples of **joint Honours** degrees in which you study psychology and one other subject to the same level. Examples include Psychology and Management, Psychology and Mathematics, Psychology and Sociology. This kind of programme enables you to study two subjects in depth, but you may need to check whether the overall workload is slightly higher than studying for a single Honours degree.

By contrast, modular degrees offer a range of different subject modules often linked by a unifying theme. Often called '**combined degrees**' they are typically provided by institutes and colleges of higher education and enable students to study psychology alongside other subjects in the social sciences or humanities. With joint degrees, and combined degrees in particular, it is important for applicants to check to see if the degree course is recognised by the British Psychological Society (BPS) and gives the Graduate Basis for Registration (GBR). Without this, it will be difficult to qualify professionally. The British Psychological Society's website provides an on line search for accredited degree courses. The address is given at the back of the book.

■ Full time or sandwich?

Most degree courses in psychology are full time and last for three years, but some last four years, particularly those in Scotland, where it takes four years to gain an Honours degree. A small number of programmes, called sandwich courses, give students the chance to spend their third year on practical placements in companies or with different psychological services or agencies. Students then return to their university for their final year of study.

Although sandwich courses last four years, they can provide students with a valuable opportunity to gain first-hand experience which helps them not only to develop new skills but also to make decisions about which career path to take when they graduate. In one or two instances courses have a 'year abroad' option and arrange for students to spend a year studying at a university outside the UK, in Europe or North America for example.

■ Degree course content

Most degree courses offer a broad-based introduction to the subject to allow for the fact that many students will not have studied psychology before. This will be followed by increasing specialisation and advanced study as the programme progresses.

First year

In the first year you will be offered introductory courses in different aspects of psychology as well as in research methods, statistics and the use of information technology. You will hear about some of the key debates in the field of psychological research. For example, how far is human behaviour learned or inherited?

Second year

Courses in year 2 will build on and extend subjects studied in the first year. You may also have to complete a series of laboratory or experimental classes to give you a practical insight into psychological research methods. The results of your second year assessment may well count towards your final degree result.

Third/final year

In the final year of a degree programme, students usually have the opportunity to choose modules or options that interest them, options which typically reflect the research interests of the staff in the Department of Psychology concerned. At the same time students will invariably undertake a major dissertation, based on a research project of their own choosing. This is a significant piece of work and the choice of topic may well have some direct relevance to a student's future career choice.

A typical course programme might consist of:

1st year	2nd year	3rd year
Methods and approaches to psychology	Research methods	Research project
Experimental psychology	Further experimental psychology	Option topics
Statistical methods	Behavioural psychology	
Social psychology	Cognitive psychology	
Memory	Developmental psychology	

Definitions

For potential students who have not studied psychology before, the following definitions may be helpful in knowing what might be covered in different course modules:

Cognitive psychology covers the relationship between the brain and human behaviour. It includes the study of memory, thinking and problem-solving.

Clinical and abnormal psychology concerns the symptoms, classification and theories of different forms of mental illness.

Developmental psychology is the study of the process of human growth and development from birth to adulthood.

Neuropsychology looks at the way the central nervous system operates in relation to the sensory processes – seeing and hearing, in particular.

Psycholinguistics involves the interface between psychology and language, its acquisition and structure.

Psychometrics is the measurement of attributes such as aptitude or personality, using psychological tests.

If you want to find out more, you can read one of the introductory text-books designed for first year undergraduates. As well as the topics listed above you may find that a first degree in psychology will also cover some or all of the following:

- Social psychology
- Language acquisition
- Individual differences and psychological testing
- Statistics and experimental methods.

■ Entry grades

As with other degree subjects, the grades required for entry to degree courses in psychology vary from one university to another. Typically, the older established universities may ask for 300–340 points, or a grade equivalent (BBB to AAB). By contrast, some of the newer univer sities may have slightly lower entry requirements. Given the statistical component of most degree courses, admissions tutors will also expect applicants to have a reasonable pass grade in GCSE Mathematics.

Further details about the grades required by different universities can be found in some of the university and college listings (page 31).

■ Choosing a university

With over 100 universities offering psychology and psychology-related courses, how do you narrow down your choice to the maximum of five allowed on the UCAS form?

Things to consider:

- The grades that you are likely to achieve – there is no point in applying to universities whose standard offers are significantly higher than the grades that you are predicted, or get.
- The location of the university.
- The facilities.
- The course.

You might also find it helpful to look at the league tables compiled by the national newspapers. Whilst all league tables should be used as a guide rather than as the definitive ranking of the university, they can be useful as a starting point if you are unsure how to start looking. In its 2005 rankings, the *Guardian*'s university guide (http://education.guardian.co.uk/universityguide) placed Oxford and UCL in joint first place, followed by York, St Andrews and Napier. The ranking is based on a number of scores, including the government's teaching inspection score, an entry score based on grades achieved by students joining the courses, staff:student ratio, job prospects and spending. The *Guardian's* website allows you to re-order the tables to reflect your own criteria, or to change the weighting of the individual categories, For example, a ranking based on entry score places Hull, Nottingham, Oxford and York in joint first place. A ranking based on job prospects, on the other hand, has Napier in first place, followed by Bath, City, Liverpool Hope, Oxford, Thames Valley and UCL all sharing second place.

03 Careers in psychology

There are essentially three main career routes for those who complete a degree course in psychology:

1| To train as a professional psychologist by completing several years of further study and training at postgraduate level.
2| To enter work or postgraduate training which builds on or relates to knowledge gained during a psychology degree programme.
3| To find a graduate-level career which is unrelated to psychology but which may reflect your particular skills and interests.

The three routes are outlined in more detail below to give you an idea of what you might expect after three or four years of study.

Professional psychology

Fewer graduates than you might expect follow this route. In order to qualify as a professional psychologist your degree course must give you the Graduate Basis for Registration (GBR) of the British Psychological Society (BPS). This is normally gained by following a course that is accredited by the Society.

Once they meet that condition, graduates will then have to start on a sometimes lengthy period of postgraduate study and practical experience to qualify for Chartered Status to enable them to practise professionally. The main professional career routes are described below.

Clinical psychology

This is the largest specialism in professional psychology. Working mainly in the National Health Service, clinical psychologists work with clients of all ages by assessing their needs, providing therapy and carrying out research into the effects of different therapeutic methods. Their clients may be otherwise normal people who may have one of a range of problems such as drug dependency, emotional and interpersonal problems or particular learning difficulties. The clinical psychologist's role should not be confused with that of the psychiatrist.

Entry to training programmes is highly competitive and you will need a good pass in your degree as well as relevant work experience. This can be of two kinds – either work experience in some aspect of clinical care or community work or experience as a psychology assistant working alongside existing clinical psychologists in a health authority. Vacancies for assistants occur quite frequently, but after working in this role there is no guarantee of gaining entry to a professional training programme, which takes a further three years and leads to a Doctoral degree. This final stage of professional training can take the form of either full-time study at a university coupled with practical experience or an in-service training programme with a health authority.

Occupational psychology

In comparison with other professional groups, occupational psychologists can work for a variety of employers and can be employed in a number of different roles. In government departments such as the Department for Children, Schools and Families (DCSF) and the Ministry of Defence psychologists can be involved in research or advisory work on the most effective ways of selecting, training and employing personnel. In the Disability Service they assess individual clients and advise on the kind of work and training which might suit them.

By contrast, in business consultancies, psychologists could be involved in the development of new psychological tests or in the design and delivery of company training programmes on topics such as team building. In large companies, occupational psychologists might introduce new systems for staff training and development, while in applied research they could find themselves working alongside engineers on the design of the interface between equipment and its potential user. In short, there are many potential areas of employment and freelance work. To qualify for Chartered Status in this field, psychology graduates need to complete a specialist postgraduate course lasting one year and in addition have three years' supervised work experience. Further details are available from the British Psychological Society's website.

Educational psychology

Educational psychologists are experts in child and adolescent development. They work mainly for local education authorities and liaise with teachers and parents in identifying and assessing pupils and students with particular learning difficulties. These can range from dyslexia to disruptive classroom behaviour. Educational psychologists may not be concerned with the treatment of individual problems, but will act in a diagnostic, advisory and consultancy role. The referral of children with special educational needs to special schools is a typical example of a situation in which an educational psychologist's advice would be sought. To qualify for this specialism requires a lengthy period of further study, training and experience.

Different arrangements apply in Scotland, where educational psychologists do not need teaching experience, but in England and Wales psychology graduates are required to complete a one-year course of teacher training and have two years' teaching experience before starting a postgraduate course in Educational Psychology. This is then followed by one year of supervised practice, making it the longest qualification period of any psychology specialism.

Forensic psychology

Often known as criminological psychologists, those in this professional group work mainly in the Prison Service, assessing prisoners in terms of their rehabilitation needs and also in terms of their level of risk. The assessment is usually based on psychometric test results and clinical interviews. In addition, forensic psychologists carry out research and put in place treatment programmes to change offending behaviour and often work with groups of offenders to achieve this aim. Some psychologists in this grouping may also appear in court proceedings to give an expert view on, for instance, the mental state of defendants.

Once again, the qualification period is three years and this comprises study for a postgraduate Master's programme, recognised by the British Psychological Society, along with supervised work experience. For details, see www.bps.org.uk/sub-syst/dfp/training.cfm.

Health psychology

Health psychologists look at the links between healthcare and illness. This can include behaviour which carries with it a health risk (such as smoking or drug use); preventative measures (exercise, diet, health checks); the delivery of healthcare; and the psychological aspects of illness, such as how patients cope with pain or terminal illness.

There are a number of accredited MSc courses for candidates who have achieved the GBR. Following this, candidates must gain two years' experience in a related field before being assessed by the BPS.

Sports psychology

Sports psychology is a growing field. Increasingly, professional sportsmen and women are using psychologists to help them to improve their performances. Many football clubs, for instance, now employ sports psychologists to work with their players on an individual and team basis. The aim of the sports psychologist is to enhance performance by improving the focus or the motivation of the participants, and to encourage a 'will to win'.

There are no specific qualifications necessary to go into sports psychology, other than the need for a Psychology degree. Further information can be obtained from the British Association of Sport and Exercise Sciences, whose address is at the end of this book.

Counselling psychology

A counselling psychologist helps people to deal with problems. Typically, these might include bereavement or relationship and family problems. The counselling psychologist usually works on a one-to-one basis with the subject, and tries to help them to develop strategies to deal with life problems. To attain chartered status as a counselling psychologist, an accredited postgraduate course or a BPS diploma is required following the GBR.

Psychologists in lecturing and research

Academic staff in universities and colleges of higher education will combine teaching activities, such as delivering lectures and running seminars and tutorials, with a commitment to carry out research. Their task is to keep up to date with the latest research findings in their particular area of expertise. They will spend a considerable amount of time making applications for research funding and, once the research is completed, writing journal articles to publish their findings. Entry to academic posts in psychology is very competitive. Lecturers in higher education are not required to have a teaching qualification but those

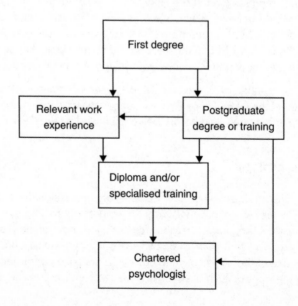

applying for lecturing posts will be expected to have a PhD and to have some published research. Lecturing posts in psychology may also arise in colleges of further education.

For psychology graduates who want to teach in schools the situation is problematic because the subject is not part of the National Curriculum. On balance it is easier for graduates to gain a place on a one-year certificate course to teach at Primary level, but even here different course centres will have their own views about whether to admit psychology graduates, who will need to prove that they have the academic interests and experience to equip them for the role of primary teacher.

Case Study

Alex chose to study psychology at degree level because he wanted a degree that would give him a choice of jobs after graduation. He did not study Psychology at A level. Coming from an arts and humanities background (he studied History, Politics and English literature at A level, and AS Philosophy), he was surprised at the scientific content of his degree course in the first year: 'I suppose that my research into the courses I applied for was sketchy, to say the least. Of course, I read the prospectuses and was able to talk about the courses at interview, but I didn't look into the detail too closely. In fact, it was not really a problem since I had good GCSE grades in the sciences and Mathematics, and they gave us lots of help on the course. At school, my friends who studied Mathematics always complained about statistics, and when I realised that I would have to do this as part of my degree course I was horrified! When we covered statistics on the course, though, it was relatively easy. It was similar with the biological content – learning biology at school was not very interesting because it all seemed unconnected with my other subjects, but making links between the functions of, say, the nervous system, and theories about how we think and learn made it much more relevant.'

■ Related careers

There are several occupations for which a first degree in psychology is a useful entry qualification because of the particular knowledge or skills it provides. For example, an understanding of individual behaviour and social development is highly relevant to careers in teaching and social work. The study of statistical methods and the analysis and interpretation of statistical results can be useful in social and market research, especially when examining the results of large-scale surveys. Any insights psycholoy students gain into the nature of individual ability and aptitudes, and the ways these can be measured, will provide a foundation for a career in the assessment and selection of personnel. Knowledge you may acquire about physiological and cognitive psychology can be applied in ergonomics, or human factors design, as it is sometimes called. Yet again, an interest in other people's behaviour or personality may well provide the basis of careers which require an element of counselling or interpersonal helping.

By looking carefully at the content of degree programmes, the research interests of lecturing staff and specialist module options which might be available, you will soon begin to see if the course is pointing its students towards a particular career direction in applied psychology.

■ Options unrelated to psychology

Many graduates in psychology will choose not to apply the knowledge they have gained from their degree course, but, instead, will use the skills they have gained in a wide range of other graduate-level careers. Approximately 40 per cent of all graduate job vacancies in the UK are open to graduates irrespective of their degree subject. With a degree in psychology, therefore, it is quite possible to train as an accountant or a solicitor, enter general management, become a journalist or work in information technology. Much will depend on your particular interests and the skills you have developed.

In studying psychology students are often surprised by the number of different skills they develop and which they can use in their work after graduating:

- **Information seeking and research skills** – the ability to search databases and employ experimental methods.
- **Analytical skills** – the ability to think critically and weigh the evidence from different research findings.
- **Numeracy** – the ability to interpret statistical data and to assess the reliability of experimental results.
- **IT skills** – the ability to use software packages for data analysis and psychological measurement.

These are in addition to the skills that most higher education students will acquire, such as the written communication skills developed in essay and report writing or the verbal communication skills used in group projects or seminar discussions and making presentations. As you can see, a psychology degree programme may help you to develop a broad range of skills which you can apply in the workplace, but you may need to make this apparent to potential employers.

Case Study

Qian Qian's parents wanted her to study economics at university so that she could work in business or finance once she returned to China, but she enjoyed AS Psychology so much, she persuaded them to let her follow a joint Honours degree in Psychology and Management. 'My parents are OK about this because I will still get a degree that is business-related, and I persuaded them that psychology will help me to stand out from other students and will also be very useful in running a business. I was lucky not only because they agreed to this, but also because my school allowed me to study Psychology at AS level. Chinese students I met socially, who went to other schools and colleges in the UK, were not given this choice.'

■ What people say

'I chose to study psychology because of its dependence on scientific research. I like the idea that the subject is constantly changing and being updated. At UCL, we are expected to keep up to date with current issues and the results of new research. I think my strength in mathematics has been a definite advantage to me when looking at research methods. I would have struggled without A level mathematics.'

Manraj

'My initial idea, when choosing psychology as a degree subject, was to have a career as a psychologist (although to be honest I had not really researched this very thoroughly). We have lots of help with careers choices at the university, and I now think that I will use my degree as a 'general' degree and try to find a job with a city bank. Although it might seem strange, psychology will be an excellent basis for this because of the need to constantly analyse information.'

Steven

'I chose Birmingham because it has a very large psychology department and I thought that this would give me the chance to look at all aspects of psychology. I also wanted to study at a university with a campus feel but that was in the centre of a city. I have chosen to do my research project on forensic psychology and I think that this is what I would like to do as a future career.'

Emma

'Unlike a lot of other people on my course, I did not study psychology at A level. I knew that I might be at a disadvantage with my application because I would find it harder to justify my choice to

an interviewer. My teachers at my college advised me to try to get some related work experience in order to strengthen my application. I worked as a volunteer in a psychiatric ward in my local hospital once a week, and I also spent time in my holidays helping children with learning difficulties. Before my interviews I did as much research as I could on the related areas of psychology. It obviously worked because I received four offers!'

Peter

'I started the psychology course at Newcastle determined to be open-minded about which area of psychology I would eventually specialise in. I am now in my third year and I have considered a lot of options but I have now decided that I will do a PhD in Clinical Psychology. Eventually, I want to work in a hospital environment but I want to go deeper into the subject before doing so. When I first started the course I had not expected it to be so demanding – I think that my idea about psychology was linked to what I had read about dreams and relationships, whereas in reality it is about scientific research and methods. I had to work hard in my first year to get up to the necessary levels of understanding, but after that it all slotted into place and I loved it'.

Gemma

'Having lived in China for sixteen years I witnessed how people ignore psychological problems. Those with mental illness are treated with medicine which does not help their mental problems and the stigma attached to needing psychological treatment prevents them from seeking help from psychologists. Moreover, psychological treatments are unavailable in some undeveloped countries. The apparently inadequate provision in China has stimulated my interest further and it has made me determined to pursue a psychology related career, possibly as a clinical psychologist.'

Sally

04 UCAS applications: writing your personal statement

General advice on completing your UCAS application is provided in another book in this series: *How to complete your UCAS application*. This chapter is designed specifically to help you plan your personal statement and to make sure it is targeted at winning a place on a psychology course. This is the only chance you get to prove that you deserve a place (or at least an interview) at the universities of your choice. It may sound obvious, but they only know what you tell them, so it's vital that you think very carefully about what to say in order to show yourself in the best possible light. The content of each personal statement is unique to each candidate – there are no rules, as such – but there are recommendations that can be made.

Universities are primarily academic institutions so you must present yourself as a strong bet. The first thing that the admissions tutor wants to know is the strength of your commitment to study. Say clearly why you wish to study for your chosen degree, especially if you haven't studied psychology before. Wanting to work with people, or liking children, is not good enough. Give details of particular areas of study that interest you and say what you hope to get out of researching them at university level. Bookshops have sections on 'popular psychology' which contain books about psychology for non-psychologists – this is a good starting point if you wish to demonstrate an interest in the subject but haven't studied it at AS or A level. A word of warning: don't try to impress the selectors by claiming that you have read degree-level psychology books, as you may get asked about your reading if you are called for interview – stick to things that you can understand and discuss. A selection of titles is listed at the end of this book in the section on psychology texts to get you started.

If you have particularly enjoyed certain parts of your AS or A level Psychology course, say so – and explain why. If you are new to the subject, give examples from newspapers, television events or controversies that have appealed to the psychologist in you. Give examples of your academic interests and explain your reasons for them.

Work experience is useful, as it demonstrates a commitment to the subject outside the classroom. If you have had relevant work experience, write about it on your form. Explain concisely what your job entailed, for example:

During the summer vacation, I volunteered at a summer camp for children with learning disabilities. This has been a most valuable work experience and I thoroughly enjoyed working with the children, particularly because I was able to appreciate much better some of the work that we have covered in Developmental and Cognitive Psychology in my A level course.

Future plans can also be included, if you have them. Again, be precise and informative. This will demonstrate a breadth of interest in the subject.

At least half of your personal statement should deal with material directly related to your chosen course. Thereafter, use the rest of the page to tell the admissions tutor what makes you who you are. What travel have you undertaken? What music do you like and/or play? What do you read? What sporting achievements do you have? In all these things give details.

Last year I went to France. I like reading and listening to music and sometimes I play football at weekends is weak. A stronger version might read:

Last year I drove through France and enjoyed visiting the chateaux of the Loire. I relax by reading the novels of Stephen King and have hardback first editions of all his books. My musical taste is extremely wide, ranging from Gregorian Chant to Robbie Williams, and I would like to continue playing the cello in an orchestra at university. I would also be keen to play in a football team to keep myself fit.

Don't expect to be able to fit everything about yourself in the limited space available, and only include things that you are prepared to expand on at interview. The idea is to whet their appetite and to make them want to meet you.

What do I look for in a UCAS Personal Statement? First and foremost, evidence of research into psychology. I will not automatically reject someone who only mentions Freud and/or relationships but this needs to be backed up with some serious reading or work experience. I do not expect students to be reading university textbooks but they should make a habit of looking at new developments in psychology on relevant websites, and reading books about, for example, how the brain works. Students who study psychology at A level can write about their research projects to show that they been thinking independently.

Admissions Tutor

05 Succeeding in your interview

You may not get called for interview at all since only a few of the universities now conduct formal interviews. However, a number of universities – usually those with the highest ratio of applicants per place – still ask students to attend a formal interview, and others combine open days with more informal meetings. If you do apply to a university that interviews applicants, don't worry: the interview is a chance for you to demonstrate to the selectors your suitability for the course. It will not be an unpleasant experience as long as you do your preparation.

■ General hints for interviews

- While the number of people conducting the interview and the length of time it takes can vary, all interviews are designed to enable those asking the questions to find out as much about the candidate as they can. It is important, therefore, to engage actively with the process (good eye contact and confident body language help) and treat it as a chance to put yourself across rather than as an obstacle course trying to catch you out.
- Interviewers are more interested in what you know than in what you don't know. If you are asked something you can't answer, say so. To waffle (or worse, to lie) simply wastes time and lets you down. The interviewers will be considering the quality of thought that goes into your answers; they will not expect you to know everything already. Pauses while you think are perfectly acceptable; don't be afraid to take your time.
- It is likely that one, or more, of the interviewers will be your tutor(s) during your time at university. Enthusiasm for, a strong commitment to, and a willingness to learn your chosen subject are all extremely important attitudes to convey. The people you meet at interview not only have to judge your academic calibre, but also have to decide whether they would enjoy teaching you for the next three to four years. Try to demonstrate your enthusiasm by mentioning books or articles that you have read, or topics that you enjoyed as part of your AS or A level Psychology course.
- An ability to think on your feet is vital. Pre-learned responses never work: they appear glib and superficial and, no matter how apparently spontaneously they are delivered, they are always detectable. Putting forward an answer step by step, using examples and factual

knowledge to reinforce your points, is far more professional, even if you are not completely sure of what you are saying. That said, it is also sensible to admit defeat: knowing you are beaten is a more intelligent thing than mindlessly clinging to the wreckage of a specious case.

- It is possible to steer the interview yourself to some extent. If, for example, you are asked to comment on something you know little about, confidently replacing the question with another related one shows enthusiasm. Don't waste time in silences that are as embarrassing for the panel as for the candidate.

- Essential preparation includes revision of the personal statement from your UCAS application. This may well form the basis of preliminary questions (which are meant to put you at your ease) and if it proves to be a mass of fabrications, the interview is doomed from the start!

- Questions may well be asked about your extracurricular activities. Again, this is to put you at your ease: your answers should be thorough and enthusiastic, but not too long! Some more specific psychology-related questions are listed below.

- At the end of the interview you are normally given a chance to ask questions of your own. If you have none, say that the interview has covered all the queries you had. It is sensible, though, to have one or two questions of a serious kind – about the course, the tuition, etc – up your sleeve. Don't ask anything that you could, and should, have found answers to in the prospectus. It is also fine, even desirable, to base a question on the interview itself. This marks you out as someone who listens, is curious and who is keen to learn.

- Above all, make them remember you when they go through a list of 20 or more applicants at the end of the day.

■ Specimen interview questions

1| Why have you chosen to study psychology?
2| What first interested you in psychology?
3| What do you understand by the word 'psychology'?
4| What do psychologists do?
5| What would you like to do after graduating?
6| What are the differences between psychology, psychiatry and psychotherapy?
7| What have you done to investigate psychology?
8| Why did you/didn't you choose to study Psychology at AS or A level?
9| Have you read any books on psychology?
10| What particular areas of psychology interest you?
11| How do you keep up with current issues in psychology?
12| Tell me about something that is related to psychology that has been in the newspapers recently.

13| New theories in psychology need to be tested: how do psychologists go about testing theories?

14| Give me an example of an experiment which tests a psychological theory.

15| Is it ethical to experiment on human subjects?

16| Describe some of the links between biology and psychology.

17| Why is a knowledge of mathematics important when studying psychology?

18| Who should judge whether someone has a psychological disorder?

19| How do you cope with stress?

20| How do you relax?

21| What are your best/worst qualities?

22| I see from your personal statement that you are interested in (insert topic/interest). Tell me about it.

23| What are you going to do in your gap year?

24| Why are you taking a gap year?

25| Why did you apply here?

26| What do you like about our psychology course?

27| What options will you choose in the second year?

28| Why did you choose a joint Honours degree?

When we interview students we want to reassure ourselves that we are not going waste a place on him or her. So, in order to convince us, the interviewee needs to have looked at our course in detail and be prepared to tell us what aspects of it are attractive; he or she should have good reasons for choosing the university (coming to an Open Day is always a plus point); and he or she should have looked beyond the degree at career routes for psychology graduates.

Admissions Tutor

■ Finding the facts

Although admissions interviews are not offered routinely by all universities, staff will try to ensure that applicants have a chance to visit the course centre to find out more about the learning environment. Some, for example, will offer group interviews in which a member of staff will lead a discussion about the degree programme, enabling applicants to ask questions about the course. Others will host open days and campus tours which provide applicants with the chance of talking to current students about the 'student experience' and viewing the university's facilities.

You should take every opportunity to visit the higher education institutions to which you are applying because, in themselves, prospectus entries will only give you part of the picture. The checklist below will give you an idea of the kinds of questions to ask when you visit a university or college to find out more about a particular course.

■ Questions you need to ask

1| About entry

- What additional information is available about the course of study, apart from that in the prospectus?
- What are the aims and objectives of the course?
- What size is the first year intake?
- What entry grades are required? How strictly are these kept to?

2| About study and learning

- Apart from courses in psychology, what other ancillary courses will I need to take?
- What are the class-contact hours for first year students?
- How much time will I have for private study?
- What are the main teaching activities?
- Over the duration of the programme, what proportion of my time will I spend in lectures, seminars, practicals, project work and placements?
- Will it help if I have my own personal computer?

3| About assessment and learning support

- Will I have a personal tutor?
- Are there specific courses in study methods?
- How will my work be assessed?
- Will my first year results count towards the final degree result?
- Are there opportunities to have coaching/mentoring from more experienced students?
- What happens if students fail their first year?

4| About career opportunities and employment

- Do present students receive help in finding part-time work to help pay for the cost of accommodation, fees, etc?
- Is the course recognised by the British Psychology Society, giving the Graduate Basis for Registration?
- Where does the degree course lead in terms of career opportunities and further study?
- What links do lecturers have with employers and practising professional psychologists?
- Are there particular course modules designed to help students with their career decisions?

These questions are largely concerned with the student experience from the perspective of academic study. Prospective students are, in addition, likely to have a range of other questions concerning accommodation, finance and the kind of facilities each university has to offer.

■ The interview itself — general tips

- Make sure you arrive early.
- Dress comfortably, but show that you are taking the interview seriously: wear smart, clean clothes.
- Make eye contact.
- Be willing to listen as well as talk, and don't be afraid to ask questions if you are unsure of what the interviewer wants.
- Be willing to consider new ideas, if your interview involves discussion of Psychology issues.
- Be yourself.
- Above all, be enthusiastic.

■ HOPE

Use the acronym HOPE to remind yourself of the personal qualities that you should try to display at the interview:

H   Honesty

O   Open-mindedness

P   Preparedness

E   Enthusiasm.

06 The universities and colleges: course details

Use this section to read a bit more about each of the places on your shortlist. They are arranged alphabetically and each one gives a contact address. The information has been provided by the universities. Information on BPS accreditation is given in each university's entry, and also in the table on pages 88–9.

You should always check the university websites and prospectuses before making an application, as the courses available, course content and entrance requirements may change.

■ ABERDEEN UNIVERSITY

The University of Aberdeen, Regents Walk, Aberdeen AB24 3FX
Tel: 01224 272090
Web: www.aberdeen.ac.uk/psychology

Aberdeen offers Psychology as a single Honours degree under both BSc and MA degree schemes. It can also be studied as combined Honours with a modern language, and as a joint Honours with Computing Science, Anthropology, Philosophy, Sociology or Statistics. The Scottish degree structure provides breadth and flexibility in the early stages, so that the final choice of degree does not have to be made until the end of the second year. Progress to junior Honours (level 3) is dependent on good performance in the levels 1 and 2 Psychology assessments. The level 3 curriculum includes courses on methodology, biopsychology, perception, developmental psychology, human memory and social psychology. In level 4 students have a choice of options, and carry out and report on an empirical investigation. Students can apply to study abroad for part of their degree under European or North American exchange programmes. The Honours degrees are accredited by the BPS (British Psychological Society).

■ ABERTAY DUNDEE UNIVERSITY

University of Abertay Dundee, Bell Street, Dundee DD1 1HG
Tel: 01382 308080
Web: www.abertay.ac.uk/Schools/SHS/psychology_info.cfm

The University of Abertay Dundee has two degree programmes that are accredited by the BPS as conferring eligibility for graduate membership with GBR (Graduate Basis for Registration). From the 2006 intake, accreditation is subject to the requirement that the minimum standard of qualification of a second class Honours is achieved.

The accredited BSc (Hons) Psychology course offers two foundation years covering psychology, research methods and sociology. Students specialise in psychology in the final two years. In addition to all the core areas of the BPS curriculum, the programme offers a range of psychology options in the third and fourth years, which may include neuropsychology, psychopharmacology, specialist topics in cognitive and developmental psychology, sport psychology, health psychology, applied psychology, psychology in education, community psychology, animal psychology, forensic psychology and clinical psychology (the latter with contributions from clinical practitioners). All final-year students submit a supervised psychology project in an area of their own interest.

The accredited BSc (Hons) Forensic Psychobiology course covers core areas of psychology with other disciplines. Compared to the BSc Psychology, Forensic Psychobiology has greater focus on psychological explanations of criminal behaviour and allows students to explore specialist subjects in forensic science and biology.

Psychology also forms a large part of the BSc (Hons) in Behavioural Science and, to a lesser extent, of the BA (Hons) in Social Science. However, these two programmes are not BPS-accredited. Note that students on the BSc Psychology, BSc Behavioural Science and BSc Sociology courses can transfer freely among these three programmes during the first two years.

The psychology department is actively involved in research and has excellent research laboratories, which students can use for their final-year projects. There are specialist research laboratories offering, for example, behaviour observation, eye-tracking, vision research facilities, human factors research facilities and speech analysis, along with a range of other experimental psychology research facilities. The university has excellent library and computing facilities, and the psychology department has its own recently upgraded teaching laboratories.

■ ANGLIA RUSKIN UNIVERSITY

Anglia Ruskin University East Road, Cambridge, CB1 1PT
Tel: 0845 271 333
Web: www.anglia.co.uk

The Department of Psychology at Anglia Ruskin has achieved a great deal of success in its short history. The teaching provision was rated as Excellent at the latest teaching quality assessment by the QAA, and the single-honours Psychology course is fully accredited by the British

Psychological Society. The main topics will include social, cognitive, developmental and health psychology as well as relevant research methods. You will be encouraged to evaluate theories and research methodologies critically and to be aware of the philosophical debates, issues and controversies inherent in the discipline. You will have the opportunity to carry out investigations using a variety of methods, including experimental work, interviews and observational studies. Opportunities are provided for group work in discussions, project work, and presentations. The final-year project will enable you to develop your skills by conducting an independent piece of research.

ASTON

Aston University, Aston Triangle, Birmingham B4 7ET
Tel: 0121 359 3611
Web: www.aston.ac.uk/lhs

You can choose between three-year and four-year sandwich BSc Human Psychology degree programmes, both conferring eligibility for graduate membership of the BPS. The four-year sandwich programme includes a twelve-month professional work placement between year two and the final year. Over half of Aston's psychology students take a placement year and it is especially recommended for those seeking a professional career in psychology, in clinical psychology for example. Students can switch between the three- and four-year programmes so a final decision about whether or not to take a placement need not be taken at application.

Psychology can be taken as 50% of a combined Honours degree in combination with a wide range of subjects. Combinations with biology, sociology, a language and business are popular but combined degrees do not confer eligibility for graduate membership of the BPS.

There is a wide range of final-year options enabling students to tailor their studies to fit their own interests and career path. Aston emphasises the human and the applied aspects of psychology and graduate employability. Aston psychology teaching is officially rated as excellent and the department has a strong record (grade 5), especially in neuroscience. As the Human Psychology degree gives you a grounding in the human and social sciences, familiarity with carrying out and evaluating research and the statistical treatment of data, a high degree of literacy and an ability to argue a case (psychology is never a cut and dried subject), graduates are able to enter a very wide range of careers in addition to professional psychology.

BATH SPA UNIVERSITY COLLEGE

Bath Spa University College, Newton Park, Bath BA2 9BN
Tel: 01225 875875
Web: www.bathspa.ac.uk/schools/social-sciences

Bath Spa offers Psychology as single, joint, major or minor BSc/BA under the combined scheme. In addition to traditional areas of study, it offers a wide range of optional modules including neuropsychology, criminological psychology and evolutionary psychology, allowing psychology specialists to develop their interests. The course is not currently accredited by the BPS.

■ BATH UNIVERSITY

The University of Bath, Claverton Down, Bath BA2 7AY
Tel: 01225 826826
Web: www.bath.ac.uk/psychology

Bath provides a four-year sandwich course in Psychology, which is accredited by the BPS as conferring eligibility for graduate membership with GBR. The course gives a grounding across the discipline, with a particular focus on social, health, developmental and cognitive psychology. Students will also be expected to take courses from the following options: sociology and social policy, a modern language or biology. Final year options can be all psychology or a combination from the above options. These are taught by staff who are actively researching in these areas. Examples currently include economic and political psychology, health and artificial intelligence, controversies in cognition. Assessment is approximately 50% coursework and 50% examination.

The department emphasises the importance of training students in marketable and transferable skills, and students are required to spend their third year on placements (probably unpaid) in one of a wide range of settings within professional psychology (for example clinical, educational, occupational or research) either in the UK or overseas. Most final year dissertations arise out of research work done during the placement. Students find the placement year invaluable as a preparation for career choice.

■ UNIVERSITY OF BEDFORDSHIRE

Park Square, Luton, Bedfordshire, LU1 3JV
Tel: 01582 489 286
Web: www.beds.ac.uk

Psychology has gained accreditation by the British Psychological Society (BPS) for all undergraduate courses (accreditation for the BSc Psychology and Criminal Behaviour is being sought) and for the MSc Health Psychology. Furthermore, the Quality Assurance Agency rated the teaching quality of all courses 'excellent'.

The Department has an international staff body with extensive research and teaching interests in all aspects of psychology, but with a particular emphasis on important and exciting areas such as health and mental health psychology and the psychology of learning.

■ QUEEN'S UNIVERSITY OF BELFAST

Queen's University of Belfast, University Road, Belfast, Northern Ireland BT7 1NN
Tel: 028 902 45133
Web: www.psych.qub.ac.uk

The subject review of psychology rated the teaching quality of Psychology at Queen's as 'excellent', awarding a maximum score of 24. Students follow a three-year degree programme leading to an Honours degree in Psychology (accredited by the BPS). The school has extensive computing facilities for students. It has specialised teaching facilities for cognitive, perception, social, developmental, psychobiological, and sport and exercise psychology, and animal behaviour. The school has close links with local hospitals and schools where many students undertake projects. The school offers opportunities to study a wide variety of topics covering the breadth of the discipline.

■ UNIVERSITY OF BIRMINGHAM

The University of Birmingham, Edgbaston, Birmingham B15 2TT
Tel: 0121 414 3344
Web: www.bham.ac.uk/psychology

Birmingham's School of Psychology is a strong department with a top research rating of 5* and an 'excellent' rating of teaching and learning of 23/24. The school has close relationships with local hospitals, clinics, schools, industrial companies and departments of local and national government. The single Honours BSc degree is structured so that for the first two years students follow a common programme in the core areas of psychology, while the final year allows some specialisation in areas of interest. The course is accredited by the BPS.

■ BOLTON UNIVERSITY

The University of Bolton, Dean Road, Bolton, BL3 5AB
Tel: 01204 903903
Web: www.bolton.ac.uk/pls

The University of Bolton offers single Honours courses in Criminological and Forensic Psychology, Counselling and Psychology, and Sport and Exercise Psychology. It also offers a BSc (Hons) Psychology course that may be studied in single, major or joint modes. All these courses are accredited by the BPS as conferring eligibility for graduate membership with GBR. The modular degree scheme offers students both mandatory and optional modules. Students study six modules each year (three per semester), which cover all aspects of psychology. In the final year each student conducts an individual research project as well as studying specialised modules. Teaching and research accommodation includes lecture theatres, laboratories, computer suites and a video laboratory.

■ BOURNEMOUTH UNIVERSITY

Bournemouth University, Studland House, 12 Christchurch Road, Bournemouth, Dorset BH1 3NA
Tel: 01202 524111
Web: www.dec.bournemouth.ac.uk

It is important today that those who are interested in human behaviour know something about technological systems – how they can be used to help people, and how their design can be improved to this end. Conversely, people of a more technological inclination need to know something about the people who will use or otherwise be affected by their designs. The three-year BSc Applied Psychology and Computing course examines the interaction of psychological and computing factors in the development of effective, safe and satisfying computer systems. The university is currently seeking BPS accreditation for this programme.

■ BRADFORD UNIVERSITY

University of Bradford, Bradford, West Yorkshire BD7 1DP
Tel: 01274 233515
Email: psychology-admissions@bradford.ac.uk
Web: www.bradford.ac.uk/acad/psychology

The University of Bradford offers a number of Psychology degrees. The BSc (Hons)/BA Psychology programme is accredited by the BPS as conferring eligibility for graduate membership with GBR. As a student of Psychology at Bradford you will develop many skills that will allow you to understand the brain, society and the individuals that exist around you on a daily basis. These skills will be developed in the Centre of Psychology Studies' new purpose-built laboratories which include: Language and Cognitive Psychology laboratory; an Experimental Cubicle Suite, equipped with PC and experiment-generation software; Interview Suite; and an Observation Suite with two-way mirror and digital image/audio equipment. The course structure ensures a broad coverage of Psychology and some of the exciting options that you may wish to study include: Forensic Psychology, Psychological Disorders and Treatment Interventions, Advanced Issues in Neuropsychology and Evolutionary Psychology. Bradford also offers BA courses in: Psychology and Crime; Psychology and Management; Sociology and Psychology and Interdisciplinary Human Studies. These courses are not currently accredited by the BPS.

BRISTOL UNIVERSITY

University of Bristol, Senate House, Bristol BS8 1TH
Tel: 0117 928 9000
Web: http://psychology.psy.bris.ac.uk

The Bristol Psychology Department has active links with other departments including child health and sport, exercise and health sciences and with the Burden Neurological Institute. Bristol offers a BSc in Experimental Psychology in the Sciences and joint Honours degrees in Psychology with Zoology or Philosophy. Both the single and the joint Honours programmes are accredited by the BPS. In the final year, students are encouraged to present reports of projects at an annual South West Area Student Conference.

BRISTOL UNIVERSITY OF WEST ENGLAND

University of the West of England, Faculty of Applied Sciences (Psychology), Frenchay Campus, Coldharbour Lane, Bristol BS16 1QY
Tel: 0117 328 3333 (Enquiry and Admissions Service)
Web: www.science.uwe.ac.uk/psychology

The BSc (Hons) Psychology at UWE is fully accredited by the BPS, covering most of the required aspects of the curriculum during years 1 and 2. A particular strength of the course is the wide variety of optional modules available at Level 3. These currently include Individual Differences in Development; Developmental Psychopathology; Advanced Developmental Psychology; Identities in Social Psychology; Psychology of Religion; Critical Sexualities; Gender and Psychology; Qualitative Research Methods; Critical Psychology; Health Psychology; Psychology of Sport and Exercise; Psychological Issues in Mental Health; Learning Disabilities; Counselling Theory and Practice; Issues in the Psychology of Education; Issues in the Psychology of Work; Psychometrics and Psychological Test Construction; Psychology of Consciousness; Psychology of Addiction; Cognitive Neuropsychology; Perception; Psychology and Evolution; Psychopharmacology; Language and Mind. Additionally, students can opt to follow named awards in Health Psychology, Social Psychology, Psychology and Mental Health, Applied Psychology or Biological Psychology. This involves selecting module options which relate to one of the above-mentioned areas and carrying out a research project in that field. Details of other, non-BPS accredited study options which include Psychology can be found on the UWE website.

■ BRUNEL UNIVERSITY

Brunel University, Uxbridge, Middlesex UB8 3PH
Tel: 01895 274000
Web: www.brunel.ac.uk/about/acad/sssl

Students can study either for a BSc in Psychology or for a BSc joint Honours combining Psychology with Sociology or Social Anthropology. Both single and joint Honours Psychology degrees are BPS accredited. The early stage of the course involves a multidisciplinary approach which is followed by opportunities to specialise. Teaching is heavily influenced by research interests of staff. Both three-year full-time and four-year thin-sandwich modes of study are available. The thin-sandwich degree is designed to link academic theory with work experience gained over two separate placements. The department helps students find suitable placements, some of which are paid. However, students are also encouraged to pursue their own placements, particularly if they would like to go abroad.

■ BUCKINGHAM UNIVERSITY

University of Buckingham, Hunter Street, Buckingham MK18 1EG
Tel: 01280 814080
Web: www.buckingham.ac.uk/psychology

The Department of Psychology at Buckingham offers Psychology either as a single honours BSc course or combined with a minor subject. Minor options are Business Studies, Marketing, Information Systems, Media Communications, English Literature, Socio-Legal Studies, French, Spanish and English Language Studies. Degree courses have start dates in January (two years' 'duration with four terms per year) or September (two years and three months' duration, spread over nine terms). The department accepts many mature and overseas students. Courses are not currently BPS accredited but Buckingham graduates have successfully obtained BPS GBR through conversion courses or the BPS in-house exams.

■ BUCKINGHAMSHIRE NEW UNIVERSITY

Buckinghamshire Chilterns University College, High Wycombe Campus, Queen Alexandra Road, High Wycombe, Buckinghamshire HP11 2IZ
Tel: 01494 522141
Web: www.bucks.ac.uk

There is a variety of both BPS and non-BPS accredited Psychology courses available at Buckinghamshire New University. These degrees confer eligibility to register for Graduate Basis for Membership with the British Psychological Society. With regard to accredited programmes, students can choose from the generic BSc (Hons) Psychology, or more applied areas such as BSc (Hons) Criminological Psychology, BSc (Hons) Sport Psychology, BSc (Hons) Psychology and Criminology and BSc (Hons) Psychology and Sociology. These all cover the core syllabus components from the BPS qualifying exam. In addition, the BSc (Hons) Psychology offers a number of career-based option modules at level three. The dissertation in each of these degree programmes is based upon an empirical investigation.

Alternatively, students may be interested in studying Psychology and working with people but not necessarily wishing to pursue a career as a 'psychologist'. For these students the BSc (Hons) in Psychosocial Studies is offered, an applied degree programme incorporating problem-based experiential learning and modules focused specifically on social problems such as disability, homelessness, substance misuse etc.

All of the degrees are of a three-year duration and the teaching is delivered via four year-long modules per year. The teaching typically consists of three hours' taught time per module per week and each student will also have the opportunity to meet as a group with their academic tutor each week. Each module is delivered so as to include the development of transferable skills and to enhance the employability of the graduates. The University has strong links with the local community and students are encouraged to actively engage in a range of extra-curricula activities.

■ CAMBRIDGE UNIVERSITY

Cambridge Admissions Office, Fitzwilliam House, 32 Trumpington Street, Cambridge CB2 1QY
Tel: 01223 333308
Web: www.psychol.cam.ac.uk and www.sps.cam.ac.uk/psy

Psychology is part of the BA in Natural Sciences or the BA in Social and Political Sciences. The Natural Sciences course is based on general scientific training and allows you to study experimental psychology along with other scientific subjects and to specialise in it in the final year. There is the opportunity to work with leading scientists and within the Medical Research Council's Cognition and Brain Sciences Unit, a leading laboratory in psychology research. Competition for places is tough!

Psychology is also one option within the Social and Political Sciences course. Psychology is studied alongside Politics and Sociology, with a narrower focus on Psychology in the second and third years. In addition, many students participate in research projects directed by the leading researchers in the Faculty and are thus prepared for careers in research and academia.

Those who take the requisite scheme of study in psychology, either as part of the Natural Sciences BA or the Social and Political Sciences BA, are normally eligible for admission to professional courses in clinical and educational psychology through graduate membership of the BPS.

■ CANTERBURY CHRIST CHURCH UNIVERSITY

Canterbury Christ Church University College, North Holmes Road, Canterbury, Kent CT1 1QU
Tel: 01227 782659
Web: www.canterbury.ac.uk/psychology

Psychology is located within the Department of Applied Social Sciences and may be studied as a single honours programme, or in combination with a range of other subjects in the combined Honours scheme. The undergraduate syllabus is taught using a modular framework and covers areas such as: social psychology, cognitive science, health psychology, psychology in education and therapeutic processes. The course is well suited to students intending to pursue a career in psychology, as well as those seeking employment in other areas requiring psychological knowledge and skills. Both the single honours programme and the major route through the combined Honours scheme are accredited by the BPS as conferring eligibility for graduate membership (GBR).

■ CARDIFF UNIVERSITY

Cardiff University, PO Box 901, Cardiff CF11 3YG
Tel: 029 2087 4404
Web: www.cardiff.ac.uk/psych

The Cardiff School of Psychology is the largest Psychology department in the UK to have achieved the highest possible rating in the 2001 Research Assessment Exercise (5*A), and it was judged 'Excellent' in the Teaching Quality Assessment. The School offers a three-year BSc (Hons) Psychology degree, and a four-year BSc (Hons) Psychology with Professional Placement degree. Both courses are accredited by the BPS as conferring eligibility for graduate membership with GBR. The modules studied on the two degree schemes are the same, but the four-year course includes a year allowing students to gain experience of Psychology in a professional setting between the second and final year. Students take up a wide range of placements covering such domains as Clinical Psychology, Forensic Psychology, Occupational and work psychology, and research settings.

Placement positions are mainly chosen from among a large menu of possibilities that the School provides, but can also be tailor-made to the individual where there is a specific ambition.

Teaching includes formal lectures combined with practical classes, computer workshops, video demonstrations and small group tutorial work. Students receive a sound foundation in psychology with the opportunity to focus on their own interests in the final year. Excellent computing and laboratory facilities support the teaching and staff research activities which include family relationships, developmental psychology, neuroscience and neuropsychology, the effects of drugs on behaviour, motion perception, face recognition and health psychology.

■ CENTRAL LANCASHIRE UNIVERSITY

University of Central Lancashire, Preston PR1 2HE
Tel: 01772 201201
Web: www.uclan.ac.uk/facs/science/psychol

The University of Central Lancashire (UCLan) offers a flexible psychology programme that is accredited by the BPS as conferring eligibility for graduate membership with GBR, provided a minimum standard of second class Honours is achieved. There are five routes through the programme leading to a BSc in Psychology, Applied Psychology, Forensic Psychology, Neuropsychology or Sport Psychology. At levels 1 and 2 all students take the same psychology modules plus a free-choice 'elective'. At level 2, those wishing to follow a specialist route take an elective in applied psychology, forensic psychology, neuropsychology or sport psychology. At level 3 students take modules appropriate for their chosen route and complete a double-module project on a relevant topic. Psychology may also be studied as a major, joint or minor subject on the combined Honours programme (for example, Psychology and Criminology) and the major 'professional route' is recognised by the BPS as conferring eligibility for GBR. The Department also offers MSc programmes in Forensic Psychology and in Health Psychology that are accredited by the BPS for Part 1 professional training, as well as a Master's programme in Psychology, Developmental Psychology and Social Psychology. For those who already have a degree there is the Graduate Diploma in Psychological Studies (BPS-recognised for BR).

■ UNIVERSITY OF CHESTER

University of Chester, Parkgate Road, Chester CH1 4BJ
Tel: 01244 375444
Web: www.chester.ac.uk/psychology

Chester offers Psychology in single and combined Honours degrees, the latter with a wide range of subject combinations in arts, humanities, science and health. The degrees are modular and particular routes in single and combined Honours degrees are accredited by the BPS as conferring eligibility for graduate membership with GBR. Core modules are completed in five semesters and the final semester offers a wide choice of optional modules. Stress is placed on practical work and research methods, and many modules have an applied slant, for example looking at the contribution of psychology to real-world problems, through educational, organisational and forensic psychology.

■ CITY UNIVERSITY

City University, Northampton Square, London EC1V 0HB
Tel: 020 7040 5060
Web: www.city.ac.uk/psychology

The Department of Psychology, which is within the School of Social Sciences, offers a single Honours degree in Psychology. Psychology does not contribute to any joint Honours degrees within the School. In the first year students take introductory courses in a range of areas in psychology, as well as one elective module from outside psychology. The second year provides a thorough grounding in the principal areas of psychology, and the third year offers a range of elective modules from both theoretical and applied areas of psychology. The degree is accredited by the BPS as conferring eligibility for graduate membership with GBR. It is currently ranked in the top 15 providers for student satisfaction in the most recent National Student Survey.

■ COVENTRY UNIVERSITY

Coventry University, Priory Street, Coventry CV1 5FB
Tel: 024 7688 7688
Web: www.coventry.ac.uk/psychology

Three honours degrees are offered: Psychology*, Psychology and Criminology* and Sport Psychology**. These share the common core areas of BPS recognised degrees as well as a module from the CU Add+vantage scheme and a skills module designed to enhance employability. Psychology at Coventry University covers a broad range of specialist and applied areas, including gender and culture, anomalous experience, psychopathology, forensic and health psychology. The Department has a strong research profile, and actively encourages student research to conference and publication level. While the BSc (Hons) Sport Psychology is the first stage towards qualification as a sport psychologist, all three undergraduate course share a common core permitting graduates to choose from a range of professional careers, and many graduates progress to the

Health or Forensic MSc programmes. The Department emphasises career development and the varied and innovative teaching, learning and assessment methods develop a wide range of transferable skills highly valued by employers. The student-centred approach to learning is supported by a strong tutorial system and by CUOnline – an exciting interactive learning environment. A Graduate Certificate and a Graduate Diploma* are also offered for students, including international students, who wish to have GBR, but have little or no psychology from their previous programme.

*Provides eligibility for the Graduate Basis of Registration
**Subject to approval

■ DE MONTFORT UNIVERSITY

De Montfort University, The Gateway, Leicester LE1 9BH
Tel: 0116 255 1551
Web: www.dmu.ac.uk/faculties/hls

De Montfort University offers a BSc (Hons) in Human Psychology as well as joint Honours degrees in Psychology. The aim of Human Psychology single Honours programme is to provide students with an insight into the human mind, human abilities and human behaviour. The joint Honours degrees offer students programmes combining psychology with other subjects. The Psychology syllabus covers areas such as cultural psychology, counselling psychology, criminological and forensic psychology, health psychology and the psychology of addiction. Assessment methods vary from critical reviews of journal articles, multiple-choice exams and practical work to the traditional essay and exam formats. The single Honours BSc in Human Psychology is accredited by the BPS as conferring eligibility for graduate membership with GBR, but joint courses are not.

■ DERBY UNIVERSITY

University of Derby, Kedleston Road, Derby DE22 1GB
Tel: 01332 590500
Web: www.derby.ac.uk

Derby offers a BSc Psychology degree, a BSc in Psychology and Counselling Studies and Psychology pathways within the university's joint Honours scheme taught on the Derby campus. A BSc Applied Psychology is available as an online distance learning course. All can be taken full- or part-time. BSc Psychology, BSc Psychology and Counselling Studies and BSc Applied Psychology are all accredited by the British Psychological Society as providing eligibility for graduate membership with GBR. Students who take psychology as part of a joint Honours degree are also eligible for GBR, provided they take psychology as a major subject.

41

Courses are offered on a modular basis, and a variety of assessment methods are used, matched to the content of the module. Psychology teaching covers the main theories and methods of contemporary psychology. Many modules include some practical work.

■ DUNDEE UNIVERSITY

The University, Dundee DD1 4HN
Tel: 01382 223181
Web: www.dundee.ac.uk/psychology

Psychology may be taken in the Faculty of Arts and Social Sciences, the Faculty of Science, the Faculty of Life Sciences or the Faculty of Engineering and Physical Sciences. Most psychology teaching is devoted to courses leading to Honours degrees (four years) and general degrees (three years). The course reflects the research interests of the teaching staff but there is an overriding commitment to present a balanced view of the subject. It is accredited by the BPS as conferring eligibility for graduate membership with GBR. Laboratory work and experience with computers form an integral part of the practical training.

■ DURHAM UNIVERSITY

University of Durham, Department of Psychology, Science Laboratories, South Road, Durham DH1 3LE
Tel: 0191 334 3240
Web: www.dur.ac.uk/psychology

The Department of Psychology offers single Honours degrees in Psychology as well as participating in Natural Science, combined Honours and joint Honours degrees. The department also offers a BSc Honours degree in Applied Psychology at its Stockton campus. The courses cover a broad range of topics from biological psychology to social psychology, and are accredited by the BPS as conferring eligibility for graduate membership with GBR. Members of staff are active in all research fields of psychology, with strengths in cognitive psychology, developmental psychology and neuroscience.

■ EAST LONDON UNIVERSITY

University of East London, Romford Road, London E15 4LZ
Tel: 020 8590 7722
Web: www.uel.ac.uk/psychology

Available full time and part time and in both the day and evening, the BSc course (BPS accredited) offers a wide choice of specialist study including: psychology of mental health, cognitive neuropsychology, drugs and behaviour, counselling, developing minds, animal behaviour, and occupational, evolutionary and forensic psychology. The department also offers postgraduate research courses in all the main areas of professional applied psychology as well as having numerous postgraduate research students. A graduate Diploma course is also offered for graduates of other disciplines who wish to convert their first degree to one which is acceptable for registration with the BPS.

◼ EDGE HILL UNIVERSITY

Edge Hill, St Helens Road, Ormskirk, Lancs L39 4QP
Tel: 01695 575171
Web: www.edgehill.ac.uk/Faculties/HMSAS/DSAPS

The course leads to a BSc single Honours degree in Psychology, and is accredited by the BPS as conferring eligibility for graduate membership with GBR. The three-year full-time programme covers all of the major areas that feature in the BPS qualifying examination: cognitive psychology; social psychology; developmental psycho logy; biological psychology; personality and individual differences; and research methods. In the third year a number of specialist options are available, including work psychology, educational psychology, addiction studies, mental health, and the psychology of personal relationships. Students also undertake a supervised research project in their final year. Psychology was rated 'excellent' for its teaching by HEFCE in its most recent inspection. The course is taught in purpose-built psychology laboratories. A range of facilities is available, including internet and CD-ROM systems, for example online journals and abstract databases.

◼ EDINBURGH UNIVERSITY

The University of Edinburgh, College of Humanities & Social Sciences (HSS), Undergraduate Admissions Office, University of Edinburgh, David Hume Tower, George Square, Edinburgh EH8 9JX
Tel: 0131 650 3565
Web: www.psy.ed.ac.uk

The undergraduate programme in Psychology at the University of Edinburgh is a four-year course leading either to an MA or to a BSc. The degree courses are accredited by the BPS and, in addition to covering the BPS 'core criteria', Edinburgh has particular strengths in the psychology of language and cognition, health and individual differences, and is currently expanding as a centre of excellence in human cognitive neuroscience.

The first-year course assumes no previous experience of psycho
logy, and introduces students to the breadth of the discipline, including biological, cognitive, developmental and social psychology,
plus the psychology of individual differences and perception. Sec-
ond- and third-year courses extend these topics into intermediate
and advanced levels. Fourth-year students choose from a broader
range of options related to contemporary research issues. Also in
the fourth year, students carry out an original research project under
staff supervision. Through their choice of options and project work,
students have the opportunity to focus on areas in which they are
particularly interested. A practical component runs through all four
years, which gives training in research methods and statistics.

The university also offers joint degrees that combine psychology
with other subjects within the School of Philosophy, Psychology and
Language Science, as well as a BSc in Biological Sciences in which
Psychology can form a part.

■ ESSEX UNIVERSITY

University of Essex, Wivenhoe Park, Colchester CO4 3SQ
Tel: 01206 873666
Web: www.essex.ac.uk/psychology

The Psychology Department at Essex is young, dynamic, enthusiastic
and research-orientated. In its own purpose-designed building, the Department has the latest facilities for lecture and laboratory-based learning.
The degrees at Essex cover the fundamentals of psychology while at the
same time providing courses in the most interesting current research
topics within a structure designed to maximise student choice.

Both the BA and BSc Psychology degrees offered by the University
of Essex are fully accredited by the British Psychological Society. The
degree schemes are identical and cover core areas in psychology ,includ-
ing: developmental psychology, intelligence, lanuage, memory, perception,
social psychology, health psychology, and research methods and statistics.
Other degrees which may be of interest are BSc Social Psychology and
Sociology and BA Criminology with Social Psychology.

■ EXETER UNIVERSITY

University of Exeter, Northcote House, The Queen's Drive, Exeter EX4 4QJ
Tel: 01392 263035
Web: www.ex.ac.uk/psychology

Psychology is offered as both a BSc and a BA three-year programme
and both are identical in content; psychology is taught as a science
throughout. Teaching covers core areas, together with training in

carrying out research and statistical analysis. The programmes are accredited by the BPS as conferring eligibility for graduate membership with GBR. The School achieved 'excellent' for teaching (23/24, QAA Review) and is internationally rated for its research (2001 Research Assessment Exercise: 5). It also has excellent facilities, including research laboratories, computer laboratories and an audio/video recording suite. New for 2008: two joint Honours degree programmes 1) Psychology and Education, 2) Psychology and Sports Science. BPS accreditation is pending.

■ GLAMORGAN UNIVERSITY

University of Glamorgan, Pontypridd RCT, CF37 1DL
Tel: 01443 480480
Web: www.glam.ac.uk/hass

The University of Glamorgan offers a number of options for studying psychology as part of an undergraduate programme. The following degrees are accredited by the BPS as conferring eligibility for graduate membership with GBR:

- BSc (Hons) Psychology – single Honours
- BSc (Hons) Psychology – major award (which allows students to combine Psychology with a wide range of other subjects, including Criminology, Sociology, Philosophy, English, History, Business Studies and Marketing)
- BSc (Hons) Developmental Psychology
- BSc (Hons) Sport Psychology.

The above programmes cover the core areas of psychology as stipulated by the BPS but also allow for students to select modules in a number of interesting specialist areas at level three, depending upon their specific programme. Other relevant non-GBR options include BSc (Hons) in Early Years Development and Education and a range of options from the joint Honours and minor programme.

High-quality teaching is supported by a strong research culture. Academic staff are actively involved in a range of research projects which complement their teaching specialisms. These include projects undertaken by members of the Centre for Lifespan Research (launched in September 2005) as well as a number of applied research projects in the fields of sports and health psychology. Staff are also responsible for the delivery of a number of short training courses to business and research-based consultancies. This further informs the teaching on undergraduate programmes and provides students with the opportunity to see how psychology may be applied in the wider world.

■ GLASGOW UNIVERSITY

University of Glasgow, Glasgow G12 8QQ
Tel: 0141 330 5089
Web: www.psy.gla.ac.uk

Psychology is a scientific subject with an emphasis on how the brain controls behaviour and experience. Psychology is offered in the faculties of Arts (MA), Science (BSc) and Social Sciences (MA SocSci), the faculty being determined by the subjects students choose to combine with psychology. The faculty students enter affects the subjects they will study alongside psychology in the first two years of the course. The Honours course is taken over four years and can be either single Honours or joint Honours, with a variety of combinations possible. Both the single and joint Honours courses are accredited by the BPS as conferring eligibility for graduate membership.

All core areas of psychology are covered, together with statistics and experimental design as well as other topic areas which reflect the expertise and research areas of the staff. In the final year students carry out an independent research project. The department has a strong research record in various areas, including perception, neuroscience, addictions, language and cognitive science. In the recent Teaching Quality Assurance Assessment the department received an 'excellent' and the last Research Assessment Exercise awarded the department the elite 5* rating.

■ GLASGOW CALEDONIAN UNIVERSITY

Glasgow Caledonian University, Cowcaddens Road, Glasgow G4 0BA
Tel: 0141 331 3000
Web: www.gcal.ac.uk/sls/psychology

The BSc/BSc (Hons) Psychology programme provides a rewarding and challenging undergraduate education in psychology while allowing students to select modules from complementary non-psychology subject areas.

In years 1 and 2, the study of psychology is balanced with options chosen from a range of designated subject areas including sociology, politics, history, economics, marketing, media studies, biology, chemistry, physics, mathematics, environmental studies and European languages. In years 3 and 4, students can specialise entirely in psychology or continue to study another subject area if they wish to do so.

All students who successfully complete each level of the programme are eligible to proceed to Honours if they wish, without further selection. The Honours programme is accredited by the BPS as conferring eligibility for graduate membership with GBR.

■ UNIVERSITY OF GLOUCESTERSHIRE

School of Health and Social Sciences, University of Gloucestershire, Francis Close Hall, Swindon Road, Cheltenham, Gloucestershire GL50 4AZ
Tel: 01242 714551
Web: www.glos.ac.uk

Psychology is available as a single Honours BSc or joint Honours BSc/BA combining with a wide range of subjects, including biology and criminology. Provided you follow a specified route, both programmes are accredited as conferring eligibility for the Graduate Basis for Registration with the British Psychological Society. Gloucestershire's psychology provision was voted top of all UK institutions for student satisfaction in 2007.

■ GREENWICH UNIVERSITY

University of Greenwich, School of Health and Social Care, Avery Hill Campus, Avery Hill Road, London SE9 2UG
Tel: 020 8331 7642
Web: www.gre.ac.uk/schools/health

Psychology can be studied as a single Honours subject (BSc Psychology) or as a major with a minor in Counselling (BSc Psychology with Counselling). The BSc Psychology degree is accredited by the BPS as conferring eligibility for graduate membership with GBR. The first year of study comprises two core courses in psychology alongside courses chosen from options in other disciplines (including counselling). In the second year, students cover a core curriculum in psychology which lays the foundations for more advanced work in the final year, comprising an independent research project and a variety of specialist courses in psychology and counselling.

■ HERTFORDSHIRE UNIVERSITY

University of Hertfordshire, College Lane, Hatfield, Hertfordshire AL10 9AB
Tel: 01707 284000
Web: http://perseus.herts.ac.uk/uhinfo/schools/psy

The first year of the BSc (Hons) Psychology course lays a strong foundation in core areas of empirical psychology. Modules in applied developmental and social psychology in the second year underpin a choice of final-year option courses. In the final year, students carry out an independent research project under the supervision of an experienced researcher. There is an optional short work placement. The BSc (Hons)

Cognitive Science and the BSc (Hons) Psychology with Artificial Intelligence degrees offer students the opportunity to study psychology, computer programming, philosophy, linguistics and neuroscience in an integrated programme that addresses questions of human and machine intelligence. The BSc Psychology and the BSc Psychology with AI both hold BPS accreditation.

■ HUDDERSFIELD UNIVERSITY

University of Huddersfield, Queensgate, Huddersfield HD1 3DH
Tel: 01484 422288 Admissions: 01484 472272
Web: www.hud.ac.uk/hhs/dbs/psy/index.htm

The University offers 4 courses accredited by the BPS as conferring eligibility for the Graduate Basis for Registration – BSc Hons Psychology, Psychology with Criminology, Psychology with Counselling and Sport and Exercise Psychology. All of these degrees provide high quality, broad-based education in psychology, or psychology with an allied discipline. Each course provides a sound basis of professional training in psychology as well as enabling students to develop interests in related areas. Shared, core modules comprise introductory modules in psychology and research methods, together with foundation modules in the allied discipline, where a student is taking a combined course. The second year builds on the first year with more advanced modules, while in the third and final year students have the opportunity to take specialist modules in psychology, allied areas and a research project.

Other courses in psychology offered, that do not lead to the GBR award, allow students to study psychology in a broader context. These include BA (Hons) Business and Psychology and BSc(Hons) Psychological Studies, offered at the University centres.The distinct nature of all of the psychology courses at the University of Huddersfield lies in their applied nature. Students are therefore encouraged to consider how the theories constructed by psychologists may be applied to real-world issues, and to critically evaluate the implications of such applications.

■ HULL UNIVERSITY

University of Hull, Hull HU6 7RX
Tel: 01482 465388
Web: www.hull.ac.uk/05/departments/appsci/psy

This is a three-year BSc in Psychology that is organised so that in the first-year students receive a broad introduction to psychology, and in subsequent years modules become more specialised and advanced. Hull also offers a three-year Psychology with Counselling Psychology course and joint Honours degrees combining Psychology, Sociology,

Philosophy, Criminology and Sports Science. These joint courses last for three years and students spend approximately 70% of their time on psychology components and 30% on their other subject. There is the opportunity for direct entry to postgraduate clinical psychology training from the psychology courses. The course is BPS accredited.

■ KEELE UNIVERSITY

The University, Keele, Staffordshire ST5 5BG
Tel: 01782 621111
Web: www.keele.ac.uk/depts/ps

Students combine psychology with another subject following a dual Honours degree programme which leads to accreditation by the BPS. In addition, first-year students take a one-year course in Complementary Studies which is designed to introduce a third discipline area and develop their academic skills. Over thirty combinations are available with psychology in a dual Honours programme, including disciplines from the humanities, the social sciences and the natural sciences. Criminology is the most popular subject followed by English, Biology, Sociology and NeuroScience. A modular scheme is followed in which all students take two Psychology modules per semester. Students can spend a semester at one of Keele's North American partner institutions during their second year. The School has particular strength in social research, cognition and neuropsychology, and applied psychology.

■ KENT UNIVERSITY

University of Kent at Canterbury, Kent CT2 7NZ
Tel: 01227 823961(direct line)
Web: www.kent.ac.uk/psychology

The Department at Kent was rated as being in the top 20 departments of psychology in the country in the *Guardian 2006 University Guide*. It was graded 4 in its last national research evaluation exercise, with the Social Psychology research group graded as 5*, the highest grade available. All programmes are accredited by the British Psychological Society (BPS) as conferring eligibility for Graduate Membership of the Society with Graduate Basis for Registration, provided students achieve the minimum standard of qualification of second class Honours.

Kent offers degrees in Psychology; Psychology with Clinical Psychology; Social Psychology; Social Psychology with Clinical Psychology; Applied Psychology; Applied Psychology with Clinical Psychology; Applied Social Psychology; Applied Social Psychology with Clinical Psychology; Computing and Psychology; Psychology and Sociology; Psychology and Social Anthropology; Psychology and Law; European Social PsychologyandPsychologywithStudiesinEurope.Thereistheopportunity to spend a year at a European university under the two European pro-grammes. Four year degrees include a placement where students un-dertake special project work in the NHS, the Prison Service or a gov-ernment research establishment. In the final year, students are able to choose from a range of specialist options, including cognitive, develop-mental, forensic, health and social psychology.

■ KINGSTON UNIVERSITY

Kingston University, Penrhyn Road, Kingston upon Thames, Surrey KT1 2EE
Tel: 020 8547 2000
Web: http://fass.kingston.ac.uk/undergraduate/psychology/

Psychology is offered under a modular framework giving students considerable autonomy. Tutors are drawn from different faculties. The full BSc Honours degree in Psychology and the major psychology route are accredited by BPS and the half-field route confers eligibility for graduate membership with GBR.

■ LANCASTER UNIVERSITY

Lancaster University, University House, Lancaster LA1 4YW
Tel: 01524 593698
Web: www.psych.lancs.ac.uk

In the first year, students spend two-thirds of their time studying psychology and they take one non-psychology course. Psychology then becomes the focus in the second and third years. Students are able to choose whether to graduate with a BA or a BSc, and the course is BPS-registered. There is also a variety of combined degrees, the most popular of which are those with languages. Those combining psychology with a foreign language do a four-year course with one year spent abroad.

■ LEEDS UNIVERSITY

Department of Psychology, University of Leeds, Leeds LS2 9JT
Tel: 0113 343 5724
Web: www.psyc.leeds.ac.uk

The Department of Psychology is centrally located on the University precinct. Excellent facilities are provided for both teaching and research. The Department received an `excellent' rating for the quality of its teaching in the QAA Subject Review in November 2000, and an excellent grade 5 in the 2001 Research Assessment Exercise. There are approximately

50 staff members, 30 postgraduate students and 500 undergraduate students (350 single Honours and 150 joint Honours), with a broad selection of undergraduate and postgraduate Psychology courses, which are accredited by the BPS as conferring eligibility for graduate membership with GBR. Research for the Department is grouped into three main areas: biopsychology, health psychology and cognitive psychology.

■ LEICESTER UNIVERSITY

University of Leicester, University Road, Leicester LE1 7RH
Tel: 0116 252 2522
Web: www.le.ac.uk/psychology

The headquarters of the BPS is situated in Leicester and maintains close links with the Department. The research and teaching facilities include two large computer laboratories, a video laboratory, a psychometric test library and a music research library. Research strengths are concentrated in cognitive psychology, clinical psychology, forensic psychology, occupational psychology, social behaviour, development and neuroscience. BScs are also available in Psychology with a designated subsidiary subject. At present these are degrees in Psychology with Sociology, Biology and Neuroscience. All degrees offered have graduate recognition status from the BPS.

■ LINCOLN UNIVERSITY

University of Lincoln, Brayford Pool, Lincoln LN6 7TS
Tel: 01522 882000
Web: www.lincoln.ac.uk/psychology

There are three psychology programmes – two single Honours programmes (Psychology, and Psychology with Clinical Psychology) and the Psychology major programme. The Psychology with Clinical Psychology programme follows the single Honours Psychology degree programme with additional compulsory units in clinical psychology at all three levels. The Psychology major is the programme followed by joint students. Psychology can be studied in combination with a wide range of subjects, including criminology, management, health studies and social policy. All three programmes cover the core areas of psychology, supported by units on research methods, information technology, statistics and data analysis. In the final year of the Psychology single Honours programme, students have a wide range of specialist topics to choose from. The programmes are accredited by the BPS.

■ LIVERPOOL UNIVERSITY

University of Liverpool, Eleanor Rathbone Building, Bedford Street, South, Liverpool L69 7ZA
Tel: 0151 794 2957
Web: www.liv.ac.uk/psychology

There is one psychology programme – the BSc (Hons) in Psychology – with 170 places. The course has at its core the main fields and methods in psychology and is accredited by the BPS as conferring eligibility for graduate membership with GBR. The Department has undergone considerable expansion in the last three years. A virtual doubling of staff numbers allows tuition not only through lectures and tutorials but also via interactive experimental work, mainly in individual and small group projects.

■ LIVERPOOL HOPE UNIVERSITY COLLEGE

Liverpool Hope University College, Hope Park, Liverpool L16 9JD
Tel: 0151 291 3000
Web: www.hope.ac.uk/ssss/psychology

An accredited BPS programme, psychology is offered within the BA/BSc combined modular degree. A wide variety of final year options is offered, including cognitive psychology, educational psychology, developmental psychology and parapsychology. Facilities within the department include different labs, such as cognition labs, a perception lab and an observation lab. Liverpool Hope University defines itself as a teaching-led and research-informed university. The University has the commitment to provide a quality learning experience. Practical work is as much as possible interlinked with ongoing research projects.

■ LIVERPOOL JOHN MOORES UNIVERSITY

Liverpool John Moores University, Roscoe Court, 4 Rodney Street, Liverpool L1 2TZ
Tel: 0151 2313 313
Web: www.ljmu.ac.uk/psychology

Four distinctive single Honours BSc programmes are offered – Applied Psychology, Psychology and Biology, Psychology and Forensic Science, and Forensic Psychology and Criminal Justice. In addition,psychology is offered in a joint or major/minor programme with criminology. Single Honours programmes and degrees with psychology as a major subject are accredited by the BPS as conferring eligibility for graduate membership with GBR.

■ LONDON GOLDSMITHS

Goldsmiths College, University of London, London SE14 6NW
Tel: 020 7919 7171
Web: www.goldsmiths.ac.uk/departments/psychology

This is a three-year course in which the final year offers a higher level of specialisation in selected topics including occupational psychology, cognitive psychology, neuropsychology, social psychology, psychopharmacology, psychology of consciousness and psychopathology. Opportunities for part-time study and intercalated work programmes are available within the BSc programme. The course is not currently accredited by the BPS.

■ LONDON METROPOLITAN UNIVERSITY

Department of Psychology, City Campus, Calcutta House, Old Castle Street, London E1 7NT
Tel: 020 7320 1067
Web:www.londonmet.ac.uk/ug-prospectus-2005/courses/psychology.cfm

The Department of Psychology has been offering degrees in psychology for over 35 years. The department has two locations; City Campus is located in Calcutta House at the edge of the City of London and North Campus is located in Ladbroke House close to Highbury, north London.

City Campus currently offers a broad-based BSc Psychology degree which is accredited by the BPS as conferring eligibility for graduate membership with GBR. Level 1 provides a foundation in the core areas of psychology: cognitive, developmental and social psychology, individual differences, biological psychology and research methods. Level 2 builds on these foundations in greater depth to provide an excellent grounding in these core areas. Some level 1 modules also provide general support for the transition to higher education as well as teaching skills and techniques that are specific to the discipline of psychology. Experimental work at level 1 is conducted in a class context and at level 2 in small groups. At level 3 students undertake an independent research project and select specialist options from a broad range of choices, including abnormal psychology, atypical development, environmental psychology, and cross-cultural psychology, as well as advanced options in cognitive, social, biological and developmental psychology. Students also have the opportunity to select more vocationally oriented options, such as forensic, health and occupational psychology, that reflect the extensive portfolio of professional expertise and postgraduate courses available at City Campus.

The Department also offers the BSc Applied Psychology degree at North Campus. However, this does not confer the GBR with the BPS, but is suitable for applicants who do not wish to pursue a career as a professional psychologist. Any potential student who is contemplating a future career in psychology is strongly advised to apply for the BSc Psychology degree.

■ LONDON ROYAL HOLLOWAY

Royal Holloway, University of London, Egham Hill, Egham, Surrey TW20 0EX
Tel: 01784 434455
Web: www.rhul.ac.uk/Psychology

The Psychology Department has links with hospitals, schools and businesses which can be especially useful for the experimental project carried out in the second and third years. There is a newly built teaching laboratory and good facilities including a state-of-the-art MRI scanner (cost over £1,000,000), physiological recording equipment, and closed-circuit TV and radio. The single Honours BSc Psychology is accredited by the BPS as conferring eligibility for graduate membership with GBR. At third-year level, students have a wide choice of courses, all of which are taught by leading experts in their respective areas.

■ LONDON SOUTH BANK UNIVERSITY

90 London Road, London, SE1 6LN
Tel: 020 7815 7815
Web: www.lsbu.ac.uk

The Psychology Department offers flexible single Honours courses in psychology, as well as a Graduate Diploma for students who already hold an undergraduate degree in another subject. In addition to the single Honours course, there is also a choice of pathways in psychology with clinical psychology, or psychology with child development. The Department has 3 research groupings-cognition in health behaviours, memory in applied settings, and developmental disorders, and has recently upgraded laboratory facilities, including the development of new testing cubicles, and purchasing eye tracking equipment. There is a highly successful work placement scheme which assists students into psychology-relevant voluntary work experience in clinical, developmental and occupational settings. All of our undergraduate courses and the Graduate Diploma are BPS accredited.

■ LONDON UNIVERSITY COLLEGE

UCL, Gower Street, London WC1E 6BT
Tel: 020 7679 2000
Web: www.psychol.ucl.ac.uk

One of the first British laboratories in experimental psychology was established at UCL in 1897 and it was here in 1901 that the BPS was inaugurated. The Psychology Department is now the largest in the UK and is a major centre for psychological research, with strengths in vision, cognition, neuropsychology and clinical psychology. Its experimental work is supported by three research councils and many other research-oriented bodies. The BSc single Honours degree in Psychology is accredited by the BPS as conferring eligibility for graduate membership with GBR. During the first two years, students study all aspects of the subject and take course units outside the Department. Laboratory work in the second year involves students designing and conducting their own experiments in small groups, which provides a basis for the final year project. In the final year, in addition to the compulsory research project, students may study a variety of courses such as occupational psychology, language and cognition, visual perception, social psychology and theory of mind. All candidates to whom places are offered are interviewed (overseas applicants excepted).

■ LOUGHBOROUGH UNIVERSITY

Loughborough University, Loughborough, Leicestershire LE11 3TU
Tel: 01509 263171
Web: www.lboro.ac.uk/departments/hu &
www.lboro.ac.uk/departments/ss

There are two distinct Psychology programmes offered at Loughborough University – Human Psychology and Social Psychology.

Human psychology

The Human Psychology Department offers multi-disciplinary study in biology, ergonomics, psychology and psychology with ergonomics. An important feature of the psychology programme is its situation within this well-established multidisciplinary department. Research and teaching are both highly respected – in the most recent Teaching Quality Review the Department achieved 24 out of 24, and its research was awarded a score of 4/5.

Both the Psychology and Psychology with Ergonomics degrees are accredited by the BPS as conferring eligibility for graduate membership with GBR, whilst the Psychology with Ergonomics degree is also recognised for professional membership of the Ergonomics Society.

The relationship between theory and application is a concern that runs through all the programmes. Students are encouraged from the outset to consider the relevance of psychology and to become involved in academic work that informs and develops its critical use and application. To achieve this, the programme is entirely oriented towards the study of human beings. The organisation of the degree content into modular topics also allows the opportunity to participate in subjects elsewhere in the Department and University. This allows students to tailor their degree programme to their developing interests and career choices.

Social psychology

The Social Psychology course in the Department of Social Sciences was created in 1974 for students wishing to study psychology from a social rather than a biological perspective. The course covers the main topics of psychology, including laboratory work, and also offers modules in such topics as sexuality, crime, psychopathology and prejudice. Students may take modules from the other disciplines within the Department: sociology, media and communications, and social policy. The course is accredited by the BPS as conferring its eligibility for graduate membership with GBR. The Department of Social Sciences was awarded 23 out of 24 points in its last Teaching Quality Review, and in December 2001 was designated 5A (a top rating) for its research expertise.

■ LUTON UNIVERSITY

University of Luton, Park Square, Luton, Bedfordshire LU1 3JU
Tel: 01582 734111
Web: www.luton.ac.uk/departments/psychology

The Department of Psychology was established in 1993 and is in the Faculty of Creative Arts, Technology and Sciences. In the ensuing period of rapid growth and high student demand, standards have been externally endorsed as 'excellent' in the teaching of psychology, with the provision of first-rate accommodation for both teaching and research. The Department offers a range of undergraduate BSc (Hons) degree courses in Psychology, Health Psychology, Psychology and Criminology and Applied Psychology. These degree courses are accredited by the BPS and, provided that the prescribed pathways are followed, they confer eligibility for graduate membership with GBR. The department also offers CertHE in Psychology.

■ MANCHESTER UNIVERSITY

University of Manchester, Oxford Road, Manchester M13 9PL
Tel: 0161 275 2585
Web: www.psych-sci.manchester.ac.uk

The Department was established in 1919 and was the first in Great Britain to appoint a full-time Professor of Psychology. The majority of students work towards a BA or BSc Psychology degree that takes three years to attain. There are no differences between the two courses and the two titles only exist for historical reasons. There is also a joint degree in Psychology and Neuroscience. The neuroscience element covers a range of relevant biological topics as well as neurobiology. Psychology may be studied as an option as part of the BA combined studies in Art or BA in Human Communication. The BA and the BSc in Psychology are accredited by the BPS as conferring eligibility for graduate membership with GBR, but the joint degrees in Psychology and Neuroscience, the BA in Human Communication and the BA Combined Studies are not.

■ MANCHESTER METROPOLITAN UNIVERSITY

Manchester Metropolitan University, All Saints, Manchester M15 6BH
Tel: 0161 247 2000
Web: www.did.stu.mmu.ac.uk/hpscschool

The Department offers a unique range of courses, providing a comprehensive and integrated study of the fundamental areas of the discipline, and the opportunity to specialise. All courses listed here are accredited by the BPS as conferring eligibility for graduate membership with GBR. The major course is the three-year BSc degree course in Psychology with the opportunity for named routes (in, for instance, criminology). There is also a combined Honours degree, allowing psychology to be studied as a major along with a wide range of other subjects, and a four-year degree in Psychology and Speech Pathology, which is recognised also by the Royal College of Speech and Language Therapists, thereby providing graduates with a dual qualification. Opportunities exist for part of the course to be spent elsewhere in Europe, Australia or the USA.

■ MMU CHESHIRE

Manchester Metropolitan University, Department of Interdisciplinary
Studies, Crewe, Cheshire
Tel: 0161 247 2000
Web: www.cheshire.mmu.ac.uk

Psychology is part of the combined Honours provision at MMU Cheshire. The programme is offered either as a BA or a BSc, and students need to take at least three units per year in psychology. In the final year of this programme students must undertake an independent project.

There is also the opportunity to undertake a programme in the Psychology of Sport and Exercise. This programme is designed to meet the needs of those who intend to pursue a future career in the area, and is a joint venture between the Department of Interdisciplinary Studies and the Department of Exercise and Sport Science. Students study fundamental concepts within psychology with an emphasis on sport and exercise science, and they are encouraged to explore the relationship between theory and practice and to appreciate the application of psychological principles to sport and exercise.

Cheshire is currently in the process of seeking BPS accreditation for the combined Honours course. The BSc in Psychology of Sport and Exercise course is accredited by the BPS as conferring eligibility for graduate membership with GBR.

■ MIDDLESEX UNIVERSITY

Middlesex University, White Hart Lane, London N17 8HR
Tel: 020 8411 5000
Web: www.mdx.ac.uk/subjects/ss/psy

The Psychology degree at Middlesex University was one of the first in the UK to recognised by the BPS.

Formats of study include single Honours degree, specialised programmes (such as Psychology with Criminology or Psychology, Sport and Perform ance), or as a major/minor subject combined with another discipline. By choosing an appropriate mix of core and optional modules students can follow a pathway that not onlyappeals to their interests but is recognised by the BPS and provides an excellent foundation for the many career choices available within psychology. There is also the opportunity to undertake a sandwich degree which incorporates a work placement providing students with the opportunity to gain experience in several different areas,including clinical, occupational, forensic, health and educational psychology. Students opting for the sandwich degree also earn a Diploma in Occupational Studies.

■ NAPIER UNIVERSITY

Craglockhart Campus, Edinburgh, EH14 1DJ
Web: www.courses.napier.ac.uk

The course is accredited by the British Psychological Society as conferring eligibility for the Graduate Basis for Registration. In the first year you will study psychology, sociology, effective learning, social psychology, individual differences, and social science research. In the second year you will follow courses in quantitative research, psychology of language and thinking, biological foundations of behaviour, child development, introduction to sport and exercise psychology, animal behaviour, and researching psychology. In the third year you will study lifespan development, social psychology, cognitive neuroscience, and individual differences. You will also undertake some practical work and work on two option topics.

■ NEWCASTLE UNIVERSITY

University of Newcastle upon Tyne, 6 Kensington Terrace, Newcastle upon Tyne NE1 7RU

Tel: 0191 222 5594
Web: www.ncl.ac.uk/psychology

The BSc in Psychology at Newcastle is accredited by the BPS. It explores many aspects of psychology, including human and animal behaviour, and provides the flexibility for students to specialise in areas of particular interest. Psychology may also be studied as a joint Honours degree with Biology, Statistics or Mathematics, or as part of the BA Combined, Studies degree. These are not accredited by the BPS. Newcastle has strong research areas in fields such as neuroscience, psychiatry and animal behaviour.

■ NORTHAMPTON UNIVERSITY

University of Northampton, Boughton Green Road, Northampton
NN2 7AL
Tel: 01604 735500
Web: www.northampton.ac.uk/schools_social.php

Students at UCN can study psychology as a single Honours subject or as part of a combined Honours programme which enables them to study Psychology as a major, minor or joint subject. Empirical investigation is integral to all the psychology courses, and there is progression through each degree towards specialist final-year options. These include clinical psycho logy, parapsychology, forensic psychology and neuropsychology. Provided that the specified pathways are followed, the course is accredited by the BPS as conferring eligibility for graduate membership with GBR.

■ NORTHUMBRIA UNIVERSITY

University of Northumbria at Newcastle, Ellison Building, Ellison
Place, Newcastle upon Tyne NE1 8ST
Tel: 0191 232 6002
Web: http://northumbria.ac.uk/sd/academic/psychsport

The Psychology degree has a substantial practical component and includes basic training in research methods, supervised practical classes, training in the use of standardised tests and a substantial final-year research project. It is also possible to study psychology in combination with sport science. All these degrees are accredited by the BPS as conferring eligibility for graduate membership with GBR.

■ NOTTINGHAM UNIVERSITY

University of Nottingham, University Park, Nottingham NG7 2RD
Tel: 0115 951 5151
Web: www.psychology.nottingham.ac.uk

The School of Psychology is one of the largest and strongest in the country, with excellent laboratories and IT facilities. There are leading research groups in developmental psychology, cognition and cognitive neuroscience, and computational modelling. The first and second years contain all the compulsory core modules for BPS accreditation, enabling finalists to concentrate on areas of interest. Practical and statistical modules are taken in the first two years to prepare for the third-year project which accounts for one third of the final-year grade. All students register for a BSc degree, although applicants with arts and humanities A levels, or a mixture, are encouraged to apply. Students take different subsidiary modules in their first year depending on their background. There is a joint Honours programme with Philosophy and a BSc in Psychology and Cognitive Neuroscience.

■ NOTTINGHAM TRENT UNIVERSITY

The Faculty of Economic and Social Science, Nottingham Trent University, Burton Street, Nottingham NG1 4BU
Tel: 0115 848 4060
Web: www.ntu.ac.uk/s3
Email: s3.enquiries@ntu.ac.uk

Psychology with BPS accreditation is offered as a single Honours BSc degree course and as combined Honours degrees with either Criminology, Sociology or Sports Science.

The courses cover a range of approaches to psychology, with an emphasis on behavioural science. The first year provides a strong foundation whilst the following years offer a choice of options and the possibility of specialisation. Research methods, data analysis and application of psychology run throughout all these courses. Students will gain skills in analysis, research, communication and IT. New laboratory facilities and high quality teaching and support ensure that students have the opportunity to make the most of their time at university.

■ OXFORD UNIVERSITY

University of Oxford, Admissions Office, Wellington Square, Oxford OX1 2JD
Tel: 01865 288000
Web: www.psy.ox.ac.uk

You can study Psychology at Oxford in two ways: either as a part subject in the joint Honours school with Philosophy and/or Physiology, or as a subject on its own in Experimental Psychology. Either route is accredited by the BPS as conferring eligibility for graduate membership with GBR. Decisions on selection are made by individual colleges, not by the Department of Experimental Psychology. You should choose a college which has a tutor in psychology (not available at Exeter, Keble, Lincoln, Mansfield, Merton, St Peter's or Trinity). The first two terms consist of three introductory courses. You will then be examined at the end of your second term (an examination called Prelims) which allows you to move on to Part 1 (core courses) and Part 2 (options) of the Final Honours School.

■ OXFORD BROOKES UNIVERSITY

Oxford Brookes University, Gipsy Lane, Headington, Oxford OX3 0BP
Tel: 01865 484848
Web: www.brookes.ac.uk/undergraduate/courses/psych

Within the School of Social Sciences and Law, Psychology is a three-year BA/BSc course studied either as a single Honours degree or as a joint degree with one from over 60 other subjects from across the University. It is possible to change to a single Honours course after the first year. The Department recently received an 'excellent' quality assurance rating. The course is modular and emphasises practical and laboratory experience. A range of assessments is used, including seminars, coursework and examinations. With an appropriate course of study, the course is accredited by the BPS as conferring eligibility for graduate membership with GBR. The Department also offers a one-year conversion course to the GBR for non-psychology graduates.

■ UNIVERSITY OF THE WEST OF SCOTLAND

University of the West of Scotland, Paisley PA1 2BE
Tel: 0141 848 3000
Web: www.paisley.ac.uk/socialsciences

In August 2007, University of Paisley and Bell College merged to create Scotland's biggest modern university with campuses in Ayr, Dumfries, Hamilton and Paisley. Given the new, enhanced regional status of the University the name has changed to University of the West of Scotland.

If these changes go ahead as we intend, all students enrolling with the University will, on successful completion of their programme of study, receive an award bearing the new name.

The University of Paisley offers two main Psychology programmes. Each can be taken over three years for a BA/BSc or four years for a BA/BSc (Hons). The programme encourages students to use the findings, theories and methods of psychology to explore and understand life in contemporary society. In the third and fourth years, in addition to the core elements of the programme, you can choose 'elective' modules from psychology or the other science and social science areas. It is also possible to combine psychology with other disciplines (for example biology, sociology). Paisley offers a comprehensive personal tutorial system and provides courses geared towards specific careers or postgraduate study. Both the BA (Hons) and the BSc (Hons) Psychology degrees are accredited by the BPS as conferring eligibility for graduate membership with GBR. The joint degrees are not accredited.

■ PLYMOUTH UNIVERSITY

University of Plymouth, Drake Circus, Plymouth PL4 8AA
Tel: 01752 600600
Web: www.plymouth.ac.uk/psychology

There are opportunities to study psychology as a single or joint degree and to obtain work experience under two different routes. The first way is through the Visits Programme in which students attend an organisation that does work relevant to psychology. Attendance is for one half-day per week for one semester. This programme is the first of its kind in the UK. The second route is through a sandwich placement year. Successful completion of the year entitles you to the Certificate of Industrial and Professional Experience. Both the single Honours BSc in Psychology and its joint Honours programmes (with Criminal Justice, Human Biology, Law and Sociology) are accredited by the BPS as conferring eligibility for graduate membership with GBR.

■ PORTSMOUTH UNIVERSITY

University of Portsmouth, Winston Churchill Avenue, Portsmouth PO1 2UP
Tel: 023 9284 6313
Web: www.port.ac.uk/departments/academic/psychology

The Department of Psychology offers a single Honours BSc in Psychology, a combined Honours BSc in Psychology with Criminology and several other Honours degrees with psychology as a minor. These degrees are delivered over three years with two semesters per year, but may also be taken on a part-time basis over six years. All are accredited by the BPS as conferring eligibility for graduate membership with GBR. The Psychology BSc emphasises a 'hands-on' approach to the subject and encourages links with ongoing staff research. The department has well-equipped laboratory facilities and current research interests include: child witnesses; police interviewing; primate communication; colour perception; the detection of deception; ecological approaches to intentionality; social understanding and locomotion; psychophysiology and neuropsychology. In 2008 a new course is starting in Forensic Psychology BSc (Hons)

■ QUEEN MARGARET UNIVERSITY COLLEGE

**Queen Margaret University College, Clerwood Terrace, Edinburgh
EH12 8TS
Tel: 0131 317 3000
Web: www.qmuc.ac.uk/psych**

Psychology degrees are offered over three or four years; the three-year option provides an Ordinary degree and the four-year option provides a BSc (Hons) either in Psychology or in Health Psychology. It is also possible to include psychology as part of the joint degrees scheme, either as a major, joint or minor subject, for example with sociology and social policy, or business and marketing. Success at Honours level in any of these awards confers eligibility for graduate membership of the BPS with GBR. Health psychology is a particular speciality at QMUC, although staff have a wide variety of interests.

■ READING UNIVERSITY

**Department of Psychology, School of Psychology and Clinical Language
Sciences, University of Reading, Harry Pitt Building, Earley Gate,
Reading, RG6 6AL
Tel: 0118 378 8523
Web: www.reading.ac.uk/psychology**

The Department of Psychology in the School of Psychology and Clinical Language Science offers single Honours BSc degrees in: Psychology; Psychology, Childhood and Ageing; and Psychology, Mental and Physical Health. Psychology may also be combined with Philosophy, Art, Biology or Mathematics. All these degree programmes are accredited by the BPS as conferring eligibility for graduate membership with GBR.

■ ROEHAMPTON UNIVERSITY

**Roehampton University, Whitelands College, Holybourne Avenue,
London SW15 4JD
Tel: 020 8392 3619/3278
Web: www.roehampton.ac.uk/psychology**

Psychology is a well-established and expanding subject area within the School of Human and Life Sciences at Roehampton. The Department has recently relocated to the new Whitelands College, which offers excellent research and teaching facilities in a state-of-the-art building. The undergraduate programmes are all accredited by the BPS as conferring eligibility for graduate membership with GBR. Students can register for single or combined Honours Psychology programmes, or for Psychology and Counselling. All programmes offer a diversity of topics and methods that reflect the interests and expertise of the teaching team and contemporary developments in the discipline as a whole.

■ ST ANDREWS UNIVERSITY

University of St Andrews, College Gate, St Andrews, Fife KY16 9AJ
Tel: 01334 476161
Web: http://psy.st-andrews.ac.uk

Psychology can be taken in either the Arts Faculty (resulting in the award of an MA) or the Science Faculty (resulting in the award of a BSc) within the four-year structure of Scottish degrees. The psychology components of the degrees in Arts and Science do not differ. The first two years allow students to take additional subjects which interest them and which may be quite independent of their study of psychology. After two years, students who have done well can elect to take the Honours Psychology degree either as single Honours or as joint Honours with any of a number of other subjects. The single Honours course has full BPS accreditation; the joint Honours may also be accredited, depending on the components of the psychology course taken.

■ SHEFFIELD UNIVERSITY

University of Sheffield, Western Bank, Sheffield S10 2TN
Tel: 0114 222 2000
Web: www.shef.ac.uk/psychology

The Department of Psychology has approximately 400 undergraduate students on three-year psychology courses with BPS accreditation. Special strengths of the course are neuroscience, developmental health and social psychology. There are joint courses in psychology and philosophy, as well as postgraduate courses in occupational and clinical psychology. Students come from all over the world with a range of qualifications and backgrounds. The single Honours degree in Psychology is accredited by the BPS as conferring eligibility for graduate membership with GBR, as are the dual Honours degrees, provided that at least 50% of the course is in psychology and the relevant modules have been taken.

■ SHEFFIELD HALLAM UNIVERSITY

Sheffield Hallam University, Howard Street, Sheffield S1 1WB
Tel: 0114 225 5555
Web: www.shu.ac.uk/social/psychology

Two psychology-related courses are offered – a BSc in Psychology and a BSc in Psychology and Law. Both are accredited by the BPS. The Psychology course covers health, developmental, biological, cognitive and social psychology, and gives students scope to specialise through a range of optional modules. In the Psychology and Law course, the two subjects are initially studied as separate disciplines, but in the final year students concentrate on the links and overlaps between them by studying modules such as the psychology of crime and law, and legal perspectives.

The University has research cubicles with facilities including eye tracking equipment and electroencephalography (EEG) machines, as well as a 70-seater psychology laboratory. The last Quality Assurance Agency's subject review (an independent national assessment) rated their teaching of psychology as excellent, awarding them a grade of 24.

■ SOUTHAMPTON UNIVERSITY

University of Southampton, Highfield, Southampton SO17 1BJ
Tel: 023 8059 2619
Web: www.psychology.soton.ac.uk

The School of Psychology is part of the University of Southampton's Faculty of Medicine, Health and Life Sciences. With a student body of nearly 700 students, psychology at Southampton is one of the largest Schools in the country. The undergraduate degree programme has been designed to give a thorough insight into many disciplines in psychology: clinical, health, cognitive, developmental, learning and social. Lectures are given by experts in their fields. In the most recent national Research Assessment Exercise (2001), psychology achieved the highest rating of 5A. The curriculum covers a wide range of topics to equip graduates for their future careers.

The BSc in Psychology is accredited by the BPS as conferring eligibility for graduate membership with GBR. During the BPS accreditation visit in May 2005 the BPS commended the School for its excellent undergraduate programme and resources.

■ SOUTHAMPTON SOLENT UNIVERSITY

Southampton Solent University, East Park Terrace, Southampton SO14 0YN
Tel: 023 8031 9000
Web: www.solent.ac.uk/fmas

The School of Human Sciences offers a well established single Honours degree in Psychology (BSc (Hons) Psychology), which is accredited by the BPS as conferring eligibility for graduate membership with GBR. Three new psychology pathways have recently been validated: BSc (Hons) Psychology (Counselling); BSc (Hons) Psychology (Criminal Behaviour); and BSc (Hons) Psychology (Health Psychology) for which, at the time of writing, BPS accreditation is being sought. On all of these courses you will study mind and behaviour within the main disciplines of the field (cognitive, developmental, individual differences, psychobiology, social) as well as studying research methodology. A variety of option units is available in the third year, during which students also carry out an individual project. There is an emphasis throughout the course, and especially within the third year, on the application of psychology to 'real world' issues. Dedicated laboratories and computing resources are available to facilitate practical work. Psychology can also be studied with ciminology on three pathways: BA (Hons) Criminology and Psycho logy; BA (Hons) Criminal Investigation with Psychology; and BA (Hons) Criminal Justice with Psychology.

■ STAFFORDSHIRE UNIVERSITY

Staffordshire University, College Road, Stoke-on-Trent ST4 2DE
Tel: 01782 294643
Web: www.staffs.ac.uk/schools/sciences/psychology

A single Honours Psychology programme is offered, as well as a range of other courses including Forensic Psychology and Psychology and Criminology. Psychology can also be combined with a variety of other subject areas as part of a joint Honours degree. All programmes are accredited by the BPS as conferring eligibility for graduate membership with GBR. Psychology and Counselling*, Health Psychology* and Psychology and Life Challenges will be offered from September 2008 (*these courses are expected to be accredited by the British Psycho logical Society in summer 2008). Psychology at Staffordshire has received an excellent assessment for its educational provision from the Quality Assurance Agency for Higher Education — scoring maximum grades in five of six categories. The courses offer a very wide range of applied psychology options in the final year of study. Staff are active in research across many different fields of psychology.

■ STIRLING UNIVERSITY

The University of Stirling, Stirling FK9 4LA
Tel: 01786 467640
Web: www.psychology.stir.ac.uk

Psychology may either be studied at Stirling as a single Honours programme, or it be combined with another subject (in all, there's a choice of 15 such combined Honours programmes). All single and combined Honours programmes are accredited by the BPS, so all students have the opportunity of gaining BPS Graduate Membership with GBR. Students are accepted for entry in either September or February.

At Stirling there is a strong emphasis on research-based teaching and students can expect instruction in both theoretical and practical-based aspects of the subject. This approach aims not only to provide students with a wide range of theoretical knowledge across all key areas of the subject, but also to equip them with the necessary research skills to allow them to design, conduct and report on their own research projects. In addition, in the final year electives, students have the chance to explore in detail specialist areas of psychology that may not be encountered as part of the mainstream curriculum. Recent topic choices for elective courses have included: music and spirituality, mass human conflict, community psychology, the systematic study of dreams and evolutionary psychology.

In the most recent Teaching Quality Assessment, the Department was rated as 'excellent' and achieved a grade 5 (out of 5) in its last Research Assessment Exercise.

■ STRATHCLYDE UNIVERSITY

University of Strathclyde, Richmond Street, Glasgow G1 1XQ
Tel: 0141 552 4400
Web: www.strath.ac.uk/psychology

In the first year, psychology may be chosen as one of four subjects selected from a range of classes in arts, social sciences and business studies. Students can then choose psychology and one other subject and continue their study in the second and third years. In the fourth year psychology may be studied to single or joint Honours levels. Admission to psychology classes in both the second year and the Honours year is selective. The Department has particular strengths in the areas of social psychology, developmental and educational psychology, occupational and health psychology, perceptual-motor skills, neuropsychology, psychology of language and human communication, psychology and C&IT, interactive learning, and road-user behaviour. The BA in Psychology is accredited by the BPS as conferring eligibility for graduate membership with GBR, as is the joint Honours programme, provided that the student has undertaken the dissertation in psychology.

■ UNIVERSITY OF SUNDERLAND

University of Sunderland, Edinburgh Building, Chester Road, Sunderland SR1 3SD : 0191 515 3000

Tel: 0191 515 3000
Web: www.sunderland.ac.uk

On this programme, students will be introduced to all areas of psychology as well as studying the research methods and statistical analyses that underpin psychological research. As well as this, students will be able to select optional modules from a wide variety of areas, such as evolutionary psychology, psychology of terrorism, sexual behaviour and intimate relationships, and counselling psychology.

Both single and combined subjects Honours programmes are available, both of which are accredited by the BPS as conferring eligibility for graduate membership to the BPS (although this only applies to combined subjects students who have psychology as their major award).

As well as offering a range of topic areas within psychology, based in our award-winning St Peter's campus, the programme is taught by enthusiastic and motivated staff within the Department who are committed to developing valuable and novel teaching and learning strategies.

■ UNIVERSITY OF SURREY

University of Surrey, Guildford GU2 7XH
Tel: 01483 300800
Web: www.surrey.ac.uk/Psychology

This is a four-year course in which the third year is organised around a period of professional placements so that the students have direct experience of the practical applications of psychology. It enables them to bring this experience back to the University and apply it to final year studies. There are also extensive international links with the United States or, through the ERASMUS programme, with France, Italy or Spain. Surrey also offers a four-year BSc in Applied Psychology and Sociology that stresses the integration of theory and practice – whether it be industry, urban development, social welfare, health or education. The BScs in Psychology and in Applied Psychology and Sociology are accredited by the BPS, and the BSc in Psychology also confers eligibility for GBR.

■ SUSSEX UNIVERSITY

University of Sussex, Falmer, Brighton, Sussex BN1 9RH
Tel: 01273 876638
Web: www.sussex.ac.uk/psychology

Sussex offers a single BSc in Psychology, with a unique flexible structure in which students spend 75% of their time studying core psychology courses, and can decide whether to spend the remaining 25% studying further psychology courses, or courses from other disciplines such as sociology, media studies, philosophy and neuroscience. The university also offers a 4-year Psychology with American Studies BSc, in which year 3 is spent studying at a university in North America. All psychology degrees are BPS accredited. The Psychology Department is one of the largest in the country and has excellent research facilities. It is situated centrally at the University's attractive campus, close to the city of Brighton.

■ TEESSIDE UNIVERSITY

University of Teesside, Middlesborough, Cleveland TS1 3BA
Tel: 01642 218121
Web: www.tees.ac.uk/schools/sssl/psychology.cfm

The three-year BSc Psychology course places an emphasis on 'hands-on' research experience through laboratory research classes. Core modules include foundations of psychology, biopsychology, perception, cognitive psychology, social psychology and developmental psychology. All Teesside's psychology courses (including BScs in Forensic Psychology, Health Psychology, Psychology and Counselling, Sport and Exercise Psychology, and Psychology and Criminology) are accredited by the BPS as conferring eligibility for graduate membership with GBR.

■ THAMES VALLEY UNIVERSITY

Thames Valley University, St Mary's Road, Ealing, London W5 5RF
Tel: 0800 036 8888
Web: http://psyche.tvu.ac.uk

The specialist BSc (Hons) Psychology course at Thames Valley University (TVU) is one of the longest-established psychology courses in the UK and is accredited by the BPS as conferring eligibility for graduate membership with GBR. The course includes a placement, during which students will have the opportunity to analyse the relationship between psychological theory and practice, and to gain experience of applying psychological understanding in a health, community or research setting.

TVU also offers a BA (Hons) in Psychology and a BSc (Hons) in Psychology with Counselling Theory. All of the courses allow students to gain a full grounding and explore the process of psychological research.

■ TRINITY AND ALL SAINTS COLLEGE

Trinity & All Saints College, University of Leeds, Horsforth, Leeds LS18 5HD

69

Tel: 0113 283 7123
Web: www.tasc.ac.uk/depart/psych

Psychology and Forensic Psychology are studied as a single Honours subject or in combination with marketing, management, media, human resource management, public relations, journalism, sports and exercise, nutrition and health or sociology (either as a joint Honours degree or major/minor combination). Both single and combined Honours courses are accredited by the BPS as conferring eligibility for graduate membership with GBR. The Department of Psychology has a range of dedicated laboratories and interview/observation suites. In the final year, students have the opportunity to apply their skills and knowledge by conducting an individual research project. Specialised options include: mental health and counselling psychology; health psychology; occupational psychology; forensic psychology and child psychology.

■ ULSTER UNIVERSITY

University of Ulster, Cromore Road, Coleraine, County Londonderry, Northern Ireland BT52 1SA
Tel: 08700 400 700
Web: www.science.ulster.ac.uk/psychology

At its Coleraine campus on the north coast, Ulster offers a BSc (Hons) in Psychology and a BSc in Social Psychology, both with a full one-year placement available on a competitive basis. At the Magee campus in the historic city of Derry, Ulster offers a BSc (Hons) in Psychology. All of Ulster's psychology degrees are accredited by the BPS as conferring eligibility for graduate membership with GBR.

■ WALES BANGOR UNIVERSITY

Bangor University, Bangor, Gwynedd, ULL57 2DG
Tel: 01248 382629
Web: www.psychology.bangor.ac.uk

As the third largest Psychology School in the UK Bangor employs modern teaching methods in a friendly environment that students value. Bangor won a recent *Times* student support poll, topped the 'most helpful' category in the 2007 first year student survey.

Bangor's teaching has been awarded the highest possible grade of 'excellent' by the Government's Quality Assurance Agency. That means you'll receive first class teaching from expert lecturers within brilliant facilities. Bangor Psychology is one of only 7 departments with the maximum possible 5*A rating for research quality, alongside Oxford, Cambridge and York.

BSc/BA (Hons) Psychology, BSc (Hons) Psychology with Clinical and Health Psychology, BSc (Hons) Psychology with Child and Language Development, BSc (Hons) Psychology with Neuropsychology.

In 2007 two-thirds of graduates from the British Psychological Society fully accredited degree programmes obtained a first class or a 2:1 honours degree.

■ UNIVERSITY OF WALES INSTITUTE CARDIFF

UWIC, Llandaff Campus, Western Avenue, Cardiff CF5 2YB
Tel: 029 2041 7011
Web: www.uwic.ac.uk/shss

UWIC offers a full-time, single Honours psychology degree (BSc Hons Psychology), accredited by the BPS as conferring eligibility for graduate membership with GBR. In the first year, students are introduced to core psychology subjects which are developed over the following two years. In the third year of the course, students have the opportunity to select option modules that reflect their interests in psychology or the careers that they wish to follow. In addition, third-year students undertake their own research on a psychology topic for their undergraduate project. Assessed coursework and examinations take place in all three years. All modules must be passed to gain a degree, but the degree classification depends on the results from the second and third years of the course. The degree is validated by the University of Wales.

■ WALES SWANSEA UNIVERSITY

University of Wales, Swansea, Singleton Park, Swansea SA2 8PP
Tel: 01792 513023
E-mail: psychology.admissions@swansea.ac.uk
Web: www.swansea.ac.uk/psychology

The Psychology Department was the first to be awarded an 'excellent' rating by the Higher Education Funding Council for the quality of its teaching environment. It has a strong research record and achieved a grade of 4A in the Research Assessment Exercise (RAE) for the quality of its work. Staff of the Department have a broad range of research interests and the undergraduate course is broad based and eclectic, providing a sound education in psychology. The Department is friendly and well-organised with good student support. Teaching methods used within the Department include lectures; small group work (tutorials); laboratories; projects; assignments and examinations. In a government audit, students in the Psychology Department at Swansea University were more satisfied overall with their psychology course than in any other psychology course in Wales.

Psychology at Swansea can be studied as a single subject (single Honours BA or BSc – there is no difference the psychology core course content of the two degrees) or one of a pair of subjects (joint Honours). Joint Honours degree subjects include Psychology with one of the following: Biological Sciences BSc; Computer Science BSc; Criminology BSc (Econ); Economics BSc (Econ); English BA; French BA; German BA; Italian BA; Spanish BA; Welsh BA or Law BSc or LLB. Joint Honours courses with European languages are four years long, with the third year spent abroad. Swansea psychology degrees are accredited by the BPS as conferring eligibility for graduate membership with GBR.

■ UNIVERSITY OF WARWICK

University of Warwick, Coventry CV4 7AL
Tel: 02476 523723
Web: www2.warwick.ac.uk/fac/sci/psych

Warwick offers a single Honours BSc in Psychology which is accredited by the BPS as conferring eligibility for graduate membership with GBR. It is a three-year programme offering a general grounding in method-ology and the principal areas of psychology. Thus a quarter of the degree credit comes from practical and project work, with the remainder com-ing from courses in biological, cognitive, developmental, social and ab-normal psychology. The first two years consist of core courses in these areas, enabling the third year to contain a core project and a choice of six options from a list of about twelve. Assessment comes from exams (50%) with the remaining 50% coming from essays, project reports, presentations and tests.

■ WESTMINSTER UNIVERSITY

University of Westminster, 309 Regent Street, London W1B 2UW
Tel: 020 7911 5088
Web: www.wmin.ac.uk/sshl

BSc Psychology is a single Honours degree offered at Regent Cam-pus in central London. The course provides coverage of core areas of the discipline of psychology, while the option modules deal with the application of psychological theory and research, and give insight into the practice of psychology in a range of settings. Core modules such as social and developmental psychology, personality psychobiology, in-dividual differences and developmental psychology are taken within the first and second year. There is a choice of applied areas in the third year including cognitive disorders, forensic psychology, business psychology and health psychology. The course can be taken full or part time. The University also offers a BSc in Psychological Sciences and a BSc in

Cognitive Sciences. All three degrees are accredited by the BPS as conferring eligibility for graduate membership with GBR.

■ WINCHESTER UNIVERSITY

The University of Winchester, West Hill, Winchester, SO22 4NR
Tel: 01962 827477
Web: www2.winchester.ac.uk/psychology

Psychology is offered either as single or as combined Honours programmes. After the first year, in which all students study two subjects, they may choose to study psychology as a single Honours, or as a main, equal or minor part of their degree. The single Honours and main (75%) pathway in psychology are accredited by the BPS as conferring eligibility for graduate membership with GBR. The psychology department has good community links (for example with the NHS and with schools, etc) both in Winchester and in Hampshire, and national and international research links. This is a small, friendly department with a strong emphasis on learning and teaching.

■ WOLVERHAMPTON UNIVERSITY

The University of Wolverhampton, Wulfruna Street, Wolverhampton
WV1 1SB
Tel: 01902 321000
Web: www.wlv.ac.uk/science/psychology

Wolverhampton offers three-year degree courses, all accredited by the BPS as conferring eligibility for graduate membership with GBR. These courses cover the core areas within the BPS curriculum, whilst allowing students to develop areas of personal interest, and enabling them to develop their skills as independent learners and critical thinkers. All courses are available full time or part time.

- BSc Hons Psychology
- BSc Hons Psychology in Combined Awards
- BSc Hons Counselling Psychology.

■ WORCESTER UNIVERSITY

University of Worcester, Henwick Grove, Worcester WR2 6AJ
Tel: 01905 855000
Web: www.worc.ac.uk/psychology

Students may follow a single Honours, major, joint or minor pathway in psychology. The single Honours and major pathways are accredited by the BPS as conferring eligibility for graduate membership with GBR, provided that the specified route is followed. Psychology combines well with health studies, business management, biological science, sociology and education studies. The Department has specific research interests in the areas of health psychology, occupational psychology, developmental psychology and cognitive psychology. Psychology also runs a number of taught Master's level courses: the MSc Issues in Applied Psychology, which offers specific pathway options in Abnormal and Clinical, Business and Developmental Psychology; and an MSc in Occupational/Organisational Psychology. A Postgraduate Certificate in Changing Health Behaviours is also run, as is a conversion course – the Graduate Diploma in Psychology. Psychology also offers Master's and Doctoral level degrees by research, and each year there are a number of PhD studentships available through competition.

■ UNIVERSITY OF YORK

The University of York, Heslington, York YO10 5DD
Tel: 01904 430000
Web: www.york.ac.uk/depts/psych

York's BSc (Hons) Psychology degree offers an overall coverage of the subject with particular emphasis on psychology as an experimental science and academic discipline. After studying all major areas of psychology in the first two years, students in the final year choose from a range of advanced modules, and complete a literature survey and a project. The programme is accredited by the BPS as conferring eligibility for graduate membership with GBR. The Department of Psychology has consistently received the highest ratings for teaching and research.

■ YORK ST JOHN UNIVERSITY

York St John, College of the University of Leeds, Lord Mayor's Walk, York YO31 7EX
Tel: 01904 624624
Web: www.yorksj.ac.uk

Psychology is available as either a BSc single Honours degree or a BA joint Honours degree, on a full- or part-time basis. The single Honours degree is accredited by the BPS as conferring eligibility for graduate membership with GBR. The programmes provide a sound core knowledge of psychology and how it applies to different aspects of the human condition, such as crime, mental health, child development or education. The tutors all have backgrounds in research and applied psychology. MSc Sport Psychology is also available, as are postgraduate degrees by research.

■ BPS ACCREDIATION

As outlined in Chapter 1, the British Psychological Society (BPS) accredits certain psychology courses, meaning that graduates of these courses are eligible to apply for graduate membership of the BPS and for the Graduate Basis for Registration (GBR), which is required for the pursuit of professional training in psychology and is often referred to as the first step towards becoming a chartered psychologist.

The table below provides a quick reference for checking which institutions run BPS-accredited Psychology courses. More detailed information is given on pages 31 to 76 but do check the institutions' websites too. Note that eligibility to apply for the GBR is often subject to achieving at least a second class Honours degree

BPS accredited courses.

UNIVERSITY	BPS ACCREDITED	
	YES	NO
ABERDEEN	✓	
ABERTAY DUNDEE	✓	
ASTON	✓	
BATH SPA		✓
BATH UNIVERSITY	✓	
BELFAST – QUEEN'S	✓	
BIRMINGHAM	✓	
BOLTON	✓	
BOURNEMOUTH	✓	
BRADFORD		✓
BRISTOL	✓	
BRISTOL UWE	✓	
BRUNEL	✓	

UNIVERSITY	BPS ACCREDITED	
	YES	NO
BUCKINGHAM		✓
BUCKINGHAMSHIRE CHILTERNS	✓	
CAMBRIDGE	✓	
CANTERBURY	✓	
CARDIFF	✓	
CENTRAL LANCASHIRE	✓	
CHESTER	✓	
CITY	✓	
COVENTRY	✓	
DE MONTFORT	✓	
DERBY	✓	
DUNDEE	✓	
DURHAM	✓	
EAST LONDON	✓	
EDGE HILL	✓	
EDINBURGH	✓	
ESSEX	✓	
EXETER	✓	
GLAMORGAN	✓	
GLASGOW	✓	
GLASGOW CALEDONIAN	✓	

UNIVERSITY	BPS ACCREDITED	
	YES	NO
GLOUCESTERSHIRE	✓	
GREENWICH	✓	
HERTFORDSHIRE	✓	
HUDDERSFIELD	✓	
HULL	✓	
KEELE	✓	
KENT	✓	
KINGSTON	✓	
LANCASTER	✓	
LA SAINTE UNION CHE		✓
LEEDS	✓	
LEICESTER	✓	
LINCOLN	✓	
LIVERPOOL	✓	
LIVERPOOL HOPE	✓	
LIVERPOOL JOHN MOORES	✓	
LONDON – GOLDSMITHS		✓
LONDON METROPOLITAN	✓	
ROYAL HOLLOWAY	✓	
UCL	✓	
LOUGHBOROUGH	✓	

UNIVERSITY	BPS ACCREDITED	
	YES	NO
LUTON	✓	
MANCHESTER	✓	
MANCHESTER MET	✓	
MMU AT CHESHIRE		✓
MIDDLESEX	✓	
NEWCASTLE	✓	
NORTHAMPTON UNIVERSITY COLLEGE	✓	
NORTHUMBRIA	✓	
NOTTINGHAM	✓	
NOTTINGHAM TRENT	✓	
OXFORD	✓	
OXFORD BROOKES	✓	
PAISLEY	✓	
PLYMOUTH	✓	
PORTSMOUTH	✓	
QUEEN MARGARET	✓	
READING	✓	
ROEHAMPTON	✓	
ST ANDREWS	✓	
SHEFFIELD	✓	
SHEFFIELD HALLAM	✓	

UNIVERSITY	BPS ACCREDITED	
	YES	NO
SOUTH BANK	✓	
SOUTHAMPTON		✓
SOUTHAMPTON SOLENT	✓	
STAFFORDSHIRE	✓	
STIRLING	✓	
STRATHCLYDE	✓	
SUNDERLAND	✓	
SURREY	✓	
SUSSEX	✓	
TEESSIDE	✓	
THAMES VALLEY	✓	
TRINITY & ALL SAINTS	✓	
ULSTER	✓	
WALES (Bangor)	✓	
WALES (Cardiff)	✓	
WALES (Swansea)	✓	
WARWICK	✓	
WESTMINSTER	✓	
WINCHESTER	✓	
WOLVERHAMPTON	✓	
WORCESTER	✓	

UNIVERSITY	BPS ACCREDITED	
	YES	NO
YORK	✓	
YORK ST JOHN	✓	

07 Further information

■ Useful addresss

British Psychological Society

The British Psychological Society (BPS) is the professional association for psychologists and is incorporated by Royal Charter. A Register of Chartered Psychologists was established in 1987, bringing a more organised and stricter discipline to the profession. Chartered Psychologists are bound to an ethical code of conduct which was set up to maintain the standards of psychology as a profession and to protect the public. The Society publishes a useful pamphlet' 'So you want to be a Psychologist' – essential reading for prospective psychologists – and a range of information leaflets.

The Register lists members of the Society who have reached a certain standard in education and work experience. It contains their names, qualifications and work addresses. Copies of the Register can be found at main public reference libraries and at professional organisations and certain employer bodies.

The Register is split into specialist areas such as clinical, criminological and legal, educational, occupational and counselling psychology.

To qualify for registration as a Chartered Psychologist you must:

- have completed a first qualification in psychology that is a Graduate Basis for Registration (GBR);
- have undergone a further course or supervised training in a specific area of psychology;
- have agreed to abide by a Code of Conduct laid down by the British Psychological Society;
- be judged fit to practise psychology without supervision.

For further information contact:

The British Psychological Society
St Andrews House, 48 Princess Road East, Leicester LE1 7DR
www.bps.org.uk

The British Association of Sport and Exercise Sciences (BASES)
Leeds Metropolitan University, Carnegie Faculty of Sport and Education, Fairfax Hall, Headingley Campus, Beckett Park, Leeds LS6 3QS
www.bases.org.uk

UK Council for Psychotherapy
2nd Floor, Edward House, 2 Wakley Street, London EC1V 7LT
Tel: 020 7436 3002
www.psychotherapy.org.uk

The Association of Educational Psychologists
26 The Avenue, Durham DH1 4ED
www.aep.org.uk

The British Association for Counselling and Psychotherapy
35–37 Albert Street, Rugby, Warwickshire CV21 2SG
www.bacp.co.uk

CRAC Degree Course Guides (Psychology, Philosophy and Linguistics), published by Trotman Publishing

■ General university guides

Degree Course Offers, by Brian Heap, published annually by Trotman Publishing www.trotman.co.uk.

Entrance Guide to Higher Education in Scotland, published by UCAS, PO Box 28, Cheltenham, Gloucestershire GE52 3LZ. www.ucas.ac.uk.

How to Complete Your UCAS Application, published annually by Trotman Publishing. www.trotman.co.uk.

The Student Book, Klaus Boehm & Jenny Lees-Spalding (eds), published annually by Trotman Publishing. www.trotman.co.uk.

The UCAS Handbook is free to UK addresses from UCAS, PO Box 28, Cheltenham, Gloucestershire GL52 3LZ. www.ucas.ac.uk

University and College Entrance: The Official Guide, published by UCAS (see above).

■ Psychology texts

As far as specific psychology textbooks go, any of the introductory texts found in large bookshops are fine. Those relating to social psychology are probably the easiest and most interesting to read if you are new to the subject.

A User's Guide to the Brain, John Ratey, Abacus

Body Language, Allan Pease, Sheldon Press

Dictionary of Psychology, Andrew M Colman, Cambridge University Press

Emotional Intelligence, Daniel Goleman, Bloomsbury

From the Edge of the Couch, Raj Persaud, Bantam

Introduction in Psychology by Atkinson and Hilgard, Wadsworth

Mapping the Mind, Rita Carter, Weidenfeld & Nicolson

Memory, David Samuel, Phoenix

The Moral Animal – The New Science of Evolutionary Psychology, Robert Wright, Abacus

The Noonday Demon – An Anatomy of Depression, Andrew Solomon, Chatto & Windus

Penguin Dictionary of Psychology, Reber and Reber, Penguin

Phobias – Fighting the Fear, Helen Saul, HarperCollins

QI – The Quest for Intelligence, Kevin Warwick, Piatkus

The Human Mind, Robert Winston, Bantam

Tomorrow's People, Susan Greenfield, Penguin

Totem and Talent, Sigmund Freud, Routledge

Psychologies (Magazine available from newsagents)

■ Websites

British Psychological Society: www.bps.org.uk

Psychology Today: www.psychologytoday.com

Business Psychology News: www.businesspsychologist.com

Psych Central: www.psychcentral.com